PRAYERS JESUS PRAYED

Prayers Jesus Prayed

*Experiencing the Father
Through the Prayers of His Son*

TIMOTHY P. JONES

SERVANT PUBLICATIONS
ANN ARBOR, MICHIGAN

Vine Books is an imprint of Servant Publications especially designed to serve evangelical Christians.

Unless otherwise indicated, all quotations from the Hebrew Scriptures are translated or paraphrased by the author from *Biblia Hebraica Stuttgartensia* rev. ed., ed. Otto Eissfeldt et al. (Stuttgart, Germany: Deutsche Bibellgesellschaft, 1977).

Unless otherwise indicated, all quotations from the Christian Scriptures are translated or paraphrased by the author from *Novum Testamentum Graece* 27th ed., ed. Barbara and Kurt Aland (Stuttgart, Germany: Deutsche Bibellgesellschaft, 1981).

Quotations marked *NRSV* are taken from the Holy Bible, New Revised Standard Version. Copyright by the Division of Christian Education of the National Council of Churches of Christ in the United States, 1989. Used by permission. Quotations marked *The Message* are taken from *The Message.* Copyright by Eugene Peterson, 1993, 1994, 1995. Used by permission of NavPress Publishing Group.

Published by Servant Publications
P.O. Box 8617
Ann Arbor, Michigan 48107

Cover design by Paul Higdon, Minneapolis, MN

02 03 04 05 10 9 8 7 6 5 4 3 2 1

Printed in the United States of America
ISBN 1-56955-244-4

Library of Congress Cataloging-in-Publication Data

Jones, Timothy P. (Timothy Paul)
     Prayers Jesus prayed : experiencing the Father through the prayers of his Son /
by Timothy P. Jones.
          p. cm.
     Includes bibliographical references.
     ISBN 1-56955-244-4 (alk. paper)
     1. Jesus Christ—Prayers. 2. Prayer—Christianity. I. Title.
     BV229 .J66 2001
     232.9'04—dc21

                                                                    2001006108

Prayer is the soul's sincere desire,
Unuttered or expressed,
The motion of a hidden fire
That trembles in the breast.

Prayer is the burden of a sigh,
The falling of a tear,
The upward glancing of an eye,
When none but God is near....

Prayer is the Christian's vital breath,
The Christian's native air,
His watchword at the gates of death;
He enters heav'n with prayer.

O Thou, by whom we come to God,
The Life, the Truth, the Way;
The path of prayer Thyself hast trod:
Lord, teach us how to pray!

"Prayer Is the Soul's Sincere Desire"
James Montgomery (1771–1854)

To the most wonderful woman in the world,
my wife.
My "better half" does not even begin to describe
what I have in you.

You have captured my heart, my companion, my bride,
You have captured my heart with the glance of your eyes....
How sweet is your love, my companion, my bride,
More pleasant is your love than the finest wine.

Song of Solomon 4:9–10

CONTENTS

FOREWORD

Lots of silly things have been written about prayer.

Like: "Prayer is a way of lifting ourselves." As if we have the spiritual wherewithal to do that. In fact, the very act of praying is a recognition that we *cannot* lift ourselves.

Or: "Prayer is God's psychotherapy for his children." As if prayer were merely a psychological technique. No, to pray is to enter into a relationship—the most vital relationship that life has to offer.

Or how about this one: "A prayer in its simplest definition is merely a wish turned Godward." As if prayer were about turning God into a cosmic Santa Claus to fulfill our wishes. In fact, prayer is most often about learning to *transcend* our self-centered wishes.

And on it goes, a new definition offered with every book on prayer—with a new book and a new definition seeming to come out as often as *Time* magazine. Sadly, many such books, written to tantalize and entertain masses of readers, end up saying things that simply aren't true. And the many that do speak honestly about prayer say little that hasn't been said dozens of times before.

The thing I like about this book is that it reinforces the great truths of prayer while giving us a fresh look at the topic. And the fresh take is not just Timothy Jones' idiosyncratic, very personal way of looking at prayer. Instead it is grounded in a substantive examination of the life of Jesus.

Over the last few decades, New Testament scholars have made many remarkable discoveries about daily Jewish life in first-century

Palestine. We now know a great deal about how a person like Jesus, raised in the devout home of a skilled laborer, would have been taught to pray. We have a pretty good idea about the very prayers he would have used in synagogue services, at home, while traveling, or when visiting the temple in Jerusalem. Jones has done us a service by helping us to see, through historically grounded vignettes and careful explanations, what Jesus' prayer life would have been like.

Many today wear bracelets, T-shirts, and a thousand other trinkets that have emblazoned on them the phrase: "What would Jesus do?" The idea is to let that question guide all our actions. So why not apply it to prayer? "How would Jesus pray?" Jones not only replies to that question but also answers the logical follow-up questions: So what? In light of Jesus' prayers, how should we Christians adapt his prayer life to ours—or, more precisely, how should we adapt *our* prayer life to *his*?

Martin Luther once said, "To be a Christian without prayer is no more possible than to be alive without breathing." This is a book designed to help readers "breathe deeply" as they enter into prayer. To be sure, this is not the last word on prayer. Nor are readers obligated to sign off on everything any author says about a topic that is ultimately a mystery. Yet if Jones, as a result of alerting us to Jesus' prayer life, does nothing more than to give us a broader, deeper, and richer context to our prayers, we'll all "breathe" a little bit easier.

Mark Galli

Managing Editor, *Christianity Today*

ACKNOWLEDGMENTS

Thanks to Laura and David Franklin and to Deby and Mike Nottingham for your friendship and support during the difficulties of this year. Special thanks to Deby Nottingham, Donna Wilson, and Jerdone Davis for reading the manuscript in its early stages.

Thanks to Heidi Hess Saxton, Bert Ghezzi, and the other folk at Servant Publications for allowing me to write this book.

Thanks to Linda McGinn for your superhuman turnaround time on the discussion guides.

Special thanks to Liz Heaney. If grace is a magnificent gift which one receives without deserving it, your work on this book has truly been an act of grace.

This book was written at the Delta Café on 41st Street and the Burger King on 165th East Avenue in Tulsa, Oklahoma. Thanks to the folk at both places for fueling this project with copious quantities of calories, cholesterol, and Diet Coke.

In the days of his flesh, Jesus offered up prayers and supplications, with loud cries and tears.... Consequently, he is able for all time to save those who approach God through him, since he always lives to make intercession for them.

HEBREWS 5:7; 7:25, NRSV

INTRODUCTION

The God Who Prays

Jesus prayed.

Jesus, God in human flesh, prayed.

Jesus—God in human flesh, the one in whose name you pray—*prayed.*

During his time on the earth, God incarnate prayed persistently (see Lk 21:37). He prayed desperately (Heb 5:7). Two thousand years later, he hasn't stopped praying. In fact, according to the author of Hebrews, he *lives* to pray. And he expects us to follow his example. No other religion in history includes a Supreme Being that prays—let alone a God who "lives to intercede" for his people (see Heb 7:25).

What I find even more amazing is that Jesus *learned* to pray. He didn't emerge from Mary's womb with a prayer journal in one fist and a fountain pen in the other. Jesus was equally divine and human. That means he learned to pray in the same way that your children learn to pray—by imitating the prayers that he heard. For Jesus, these were prayers prayed primarily in the synagogue and in the temple. The Jewish liturgies helped to form the prayers Jesus prayed even as an adult.

Yet most contemporary Christians have never even heard the prayers that Jesus learned and loved. In some sense, that limits our understanding of the Father who listened so intently to the prayers of his Son. I wrote this book in order to introduce you to the prayers that

Jesus prayed. Some of these prayers are recorded in the Scriptures. Others are drawn from the ancient Jewish liturgies.

Each chapter begins with an imaginative retelling of an event from the life of Jesus. These fictional narratives weave the original context and culture of the prayers into the biblical stories in order to help you not only study the prayers, but also experience them.

You will begin your journey in the temple, overhearing a prayer of expectation that echoed within its walls on the day Jesus arrived there in his mother's arms. Later, you will become a guest at a Jewish wedding, a learner wandering the hills of Galilee, a mourner at a funeral in Bethany, a nameless bystander on the Hill of the Skull.

Where will your journey end? I don't know. That's up to you. My hope is that *Prayers Jesus Prayed* will enrich your prayer life— and even more, that it will renew your understanding of the Father to whom Jesus prayed.

Function or Lifestyle?

Before beginning this journey, let's look at one more question: What separates the prayers that Jesus heard and learned from the prayers that we typically pray? For contemporary Christians, prayer tends to be a *function*—an instrument to receive something from God. For the ancient Jews, prayer was, I believe, a *lifestyle*. Prayer punctuated every chore, every ritual, every daily task. Whenever the Hebrews rolled out of bed in the morning, whenever they washed their hands, whenever they lit a candle, whenever they drank, whenever they ate, whenever they glimpsed a rainbow, they whispered a prayer. Many of the prayers were single sentences. Most were recited in specific ways.

The ancient Jews did not pray merely because they had needs that God could fulfill—they prayed because they lived every part of their lives as people who were united with God through an unbreakable covenant. Prayer was not merely a means to receive something *from* God, it was also a persistent expression of their life *in* God. Most of these ancient prayers didn't focus on requests—they focused on God himself. Their very word for prayer, *tefilah*, had nothing to do with receiving anything from God. *Tefilah* means "to discern what is in oneself."

That's why, as you reflect on these prayers, it isn't only your understanding of prayer that will increase. Your understanding of God will grow too. You will begin to see your heavenly Father and his plan not through the lenses of tradition and theology but through the eyes of his Son. With Jesus, you will experience...

...a God who delights in doing the unexpected.

...a God who defies our assumptions.

...a God whose deepest desire is to create a community that reflects his glory.

...a God who longs so deeply for this community that he was willing to endure the cross to create it.

A WORD ABOUT FORMAT, SOURCES, AND TERMINOLOGY

Reconstructing the worship practices of first-century Judaism is extremely difficult. None of the written records of Jewish prayers are from the first century A.D. Many of the records are from the Middle Ages—hundreds of years after the earthly ministry of Jesus Christ. Some phrases in the available records reflect reactions to the emergence of Christianity and to the destruction of the Jewish temple in A.D. 70.

Reconstructing the first-century forms of these prayers entails equal amounts of in-depth research and educated guesswork. The liturgies I have reconstructed are probably not identical to the words with which Jesus was familiar. Nevertheless, I have carefully researched every rendering, and I am confident that these reconstructions are reasonably similar to the prayers Jesus knew.

In their prayers and public readings of Scripture, the ancient Hebrews substituted *Adonai* ("Supreme Lord") or *Ha-Shem* ("the Name") for *Yahweh* (the unspeakable name of God, related to the Hebrew phrase *ehyeh,* or "I AM"). While Yahweh is usually rendered "LORD" in English Bibles, in my reconstructions of the ancient liturgies I have used the word *Adonai.* My purpose is to remind the reader that although the word the Jews spoke in their prayers meant "Lord," the implication of the word was the ineffably holy name of God.

I.

Knowing the God Who Delights in the Unexpected

The salvation of Israel arrives in swaddling bands.
  The Creator blesses his creation from a cross.
    The Suffering Servant begins his ministry
      at a wedding feast.

Unexpected incarnation!
  Unexpected humiliation!
    Unexpected jubilation!

Could anyone but God ever have concocted such a scheme?
  Could anyone but God ever have made it work?
    Could anyone but God ever have delighted
      in making it work?

——THE PRAYERS OF EXPECTATION——

Speedily cause the descendant of David your servant to flourish, and increase his power by your salvation, for we hope for your salvation every day.

Conclusion of the *Amidah,* traditional Jewish prayer

Now there was a man in Jerusalem whose name was Simeon; this man was righteous and devout, looking forward to the consolation of Israel, and the Holy Spirit rested on him. It had been revealed to him by the Holy Spirit that he would not see death before he had seen the Lord's Messiah. Guided by the Spirit, Simeon came into the temple; and when the parents brought in the child Jesus, to do for him what was customary under the law, Simeon took him in his arms and praised God, saying, "Master, now you are dismissing your servant in peace, according to your word; for my eyes have seen your salvation, which you have prepared in the presence of all peoples, a light for revelation to the Gentiles and for glory to your people Israel."

LUKE 2:25–32, NRSV

CHAPTER ONE

God's Unexpected Answer:
The Prayers of Expectation

The sun cast a ruddy glow across the eastern walls of the Holy City. The ancient ramparts overshadowed two pilgrims, a man and a teenage girl, as they trudged up the western slope of the Kidron Valley. They ducked through the Ashpot Gate, at the southeast corner of the city. Already, merchants had clustered along the dusty streets to hawk dried figs and salted fish, fresh olives and fist-sized lumps of bread.

When they reached the temple courts, Mary handed a swaddled bundle of life to Joseph. She slipped through a gate into the Court of Women. Thirteen bronze chests lined the court. The girl's meager handful of coins—the price of two turtle-doves—clattered pitifully in the trumpet-shaped opening in the third chest.

From the chests, Mary made her way up the stairs toward the Court of Israel. She peered through the Beautiful Gate into the temple and drank in the beauty of the massive doors, the marble pillars, the great stone altar. Her eyes traced the snowy pillars and the billows of smoke upward until they seemed to merge with the highest heaven. As Mary remembered the words of the white-robed messenger—"Your son will be great! He will rule the house of Jacob forever!"—she whispered the last line from one of the synagogue prayers, "Speedily cause the descendant of David your servant to flourish, and increase his power by your salvation, for we hope for your salvation every day." As soon as her child learned to speak, he too would learn to pray for the salvation of Israel. And, perhaps—if she had understood God's messenger—he would *become* the salvation of Israel.

One of the priests reached into a tiny, wooden cage and grasped a dove by its neck. The bird's wings thrashed wildly and its delicate coo escalated into a frantic warble. Suddenly the priest's hands jerked. The hollow crack echoed throughout the Court of Priests. Mary winced as fresh blood spattered the corner of the altar and ran along its base. The dove was her sin offering—the offering for her unholiness, for her failures, for her sins.

Another priest severed the second dove's head and pitched it into a smoldering mass of wood atop the altar. Blood trickled unevenly down the side of the altar as the priest tore out the bird's entrails and tossed them into the ash heap. He threw what was left of the dove into the fire on the altar.[1] The sacrifice for Mary's purification was over. Now it was time for the *pidyon haben*, the redemption of the firstborn.[2]

When Mary turned around, Joseph was already beside her. The priest who stood with him was ancient, with a snowy beard and eyes that seemed to stare beyond the temple courts. He smiled at Mary and Joseph and said simply, "I am Simeon."

Joseph lifted the child and spoke: "This, my firstborn son, is the firstborn of his mother, and the Holy One has commanded us to redeem him. As it is written, '*Adonai* said to Moses, "Consecrate to me every firstborn; human being and beast, the first issue of every womb among the Israelites is mine," and, "Take as their redemption price, from the age of one month up, the money equivalent of five shekels.""'[3]

Simeon clasped the child in his trembling arms and asked, "Would you rather give me your firstborn son, the firstborn of his mother, or redeem him for five shekels of silver?"

"I want to redeem my son." Joseph withdrew a leather pouch from his belt. "Here are the shekels for his redemption."

Simeon held the pouch above the child's head and looked upward. "This instead of that," he intoned. "The shekels instead of the child. This in exchange for that. This in remission of that. May this child enter into life, into the Torah, and into the fear of heaven. Amen." At this point, the liturgy ended.[4] Yet Simeon continued in a voice that burned with undiluted joy: "You are blessed, *Adonai* our God, the king of the universe! Master, now you are dismissing your slave in peace, according to your word. Now my eyes have seen your salvation, which you prepared in the presence of all peoples—a light of revelation to the nations and of glory to your people Israel."

Mary and Joseph stood silent. They could not escape the intent of Simeon's words: This baby ... the Messiah? Someone greater than the Messiah? The revelation of the living God? Before the dumbfounded couple could respond, Simeon placed a grizzled hand on the infant's forehead and conferred the ancient blessing on them: "May *Adonai* bless you and keep you. May *Adonai* make his face to shine upon you and be gracious to you. May *Adonai* lift his countenance upon you and give you peace. Amen."[5]

Suddenly, a shadow passed across Simeon's face. His eyes clouded as he looked into the wide eyes of the girl who had borne this baby. "This child," he said, "is destined for the falling and rising of many in Israel. He is destined to be a sign that will be opposed so that the deepest thoughts of many will be revealed, and ..." The priest's lips trembled. "And a sword will pierce your own heart, also."

Simeon gazed one last time into the infant's watery, wondering eyes before handing the child to Joseph. Mary and Joseph walked silently down the steps that led from the Beautiful Gate into the Court of Women. Despite the crowds around them, they felt cold and alone.

An unexpected shout wrenched the couple out of their bewildered trance: "All who eagerly await the redemption of Jerusalem, hear me! You are blessed, *Adonai,* for you have made your face shine upon your people and redeemed them!" It was a gnarled old woman, shrieking in sheer ecstasy, whirling like a teenaged bride, waving her walking stick. She repeated her refrain again, "All who eagerly await the redemption of Jerusalem, hear me! You are blessed, *Adonai,* for you have made your face shine upon your people and redeemed them!"

The crowds parted like the Red Sea around the old woman. She was heading directly toward Mary and Joseph. She waved a bony finger at the bundle that Joseph clutched against his chest. "All who eagerly await the redemption of Jerusalem, hear me," she declared in a quavering voice. "This child, this child, is the redemption of Jerusalem!"

Surely the old woman's words were insanity, sheer insanity—the redemption of Jerusalem wrapped in swaddling bands? Mary did not know whether to laugh at the absurdity of a redeemer who couldn't control his own bowels or to cry at the sword that would pierce her own heart.

In the end, she did both.

Unimaginable Glory, Implausible Package

Who would have believed that a girl with one foot still in puberty would soon have her other foot in motherhood—without placing either foot in a man's bed? Insanity? Yes. *Holy* insanity. The recognition that "God chose the very things that don't make sense from a human perspective to disgrace this world's so-called wisdom" (1 Cor 1:25, 27). That's precisely what Simeon and Anna experienced when Mary arrived in the temple to offer the sacrifice for her purification.

For decades, Simeon and Anna had waited expectantly for the crown prince of Israel to ride into the temple courts. Every Sabbath, along with thousands of other faithful Jews, they turned their faces toward the heavens and recited a familiar prayer.[6] Because they always stood when they prayed this prayer, it became known as the *Amidah* (literally, "standing"). The closing lines of the Amidah included this prayer of expectation—a prayer asking God to establish his messianic kingdom: "You are blessed, *Adonai* our God, the king of the universe.... Speedily cause the descendant of David your servant to flourish, and increase his power by your salvation, for we hope for your salvation every day."[7]

A later rabbi expanded on this expectation of the Messiah:

> If a king will arise from David's house who is learned in Torah and observant of the commands of the Torah, as prescribed by the written law and the oral law, as David his ancestor was, and will compel all of Israel to walk in the way of the Torah and repair the breaches in their observance of the Torah; and fight the wars of God, we may, with assurance, consider him the Messiah....[8]

An obscure prayer from the Dead Sea Scrolls describes the Jewish expectations for the messianic age even more clearly: "You are blessed, *Adonai*.... You will cause the wicked to be our ransom and the faithless to be our redemption. You will wipe out all our oppressors, and we will praise your name forever."[9]

The expectations for the Messiah were clear: He would be a descendant of King David, and he would establish his kingdom through political power and military might. As far as we know, that's the sort of Messiah that Simeon and Anna expected too. What they got instead was a swaddled tot who looked suspiciously like every other infant they had ever seen.

This infant may have been from the house of David, but he didn't enjoy royal wealth; his mother offered a bargain-basement bird as her sacrifice instead of a lamb. When it came to wiping out Israel's oppressors, the baby wasn't very well equipped either. He didn't have a gallant stallion, he was too small to wear armor, and the only sword in his grasp was the one that would pierce his mother's heart.

Yet somehow, Simeon and Anna recognized this infant as the Messiah of Israel. Anna called him "the redemption of Jerusalem"—the one who would end Israel's bondage.[10] As he clasped the baby against his chest, Simeon cried, "My eyes have seen your salvation, which you prepared in the presence of all peoples—a light of revelation to the nations and of glory to your people Israel" (Lk 2:29-30).

For centuries, the Jews' prayers for the Messiah had revolved around royal rulers and revolutions. In the midst of these misunderstandings, Simeon spoke a new prayer of expectation—a prayer that revolved around the revelation of God in the least likely place, in the tender flesh of a peasant's baby. "Light" and "salvation," he called this infant. Those words marked this baby as the Messiah (see Is 52:10–13; 62:11), but they also marked him as something greater.

Centuries earlier the psalmist had written, "The Lord is my light and my salvation." The prophets echoed, "Surely God is my salvation" and "When I sit in darkness, the Lord will be a light to me" (Ps 27:1; Is 12:2; Mi 7:8). Simeon saw no flash of glory, and he heard no heavenly voices. Yet he searched the face of this wriggling infant and somehow knew that his hands were cradling the Creator of the universe. He was so certain of this infant's identity that he prayed, "Master, now you are dismissing your slave in peace" (Lk 2:29). In other words, "Master, now I can leave this place rejoicing."

Somehow, not even the utterly implausible package of an infant's flesh could conceal the unimaginable glory that Simeon glimpsed in this baby. He recognized that the child was the answer to his people's prayer of expectation: "Speedily cause the descendant of David your servant to flourish, and increase his power by your salvation."

Seeing God's Salvation

If I had been standing in Simeon's sandals, I suspect that I would have given up on the arrival of God's Messiah long before Jesus showed up in the Court of Women. When Mary and Joseph made their way to Jerusalem, hypocrisy and corruption reigned in the temple courts. For decades, the high priesthood had been "high" only because it went to the highest bidder. Now, the hated King Herod appointed high priests according to his personal whims. One group of Jews, the Essenes, became so frustrated with the corruption that they withdrew to a desert compound near the Dead Sea. The Zealots formed a political coalition and tried to force the coming of God's kingdom through violence.

Still, Simeon and Anna never gave up on the promise of God's presence among his people. According to Luke, Simeon did not go to the gathering-place of God's people simply because it was his job. He went because he was "guided by the Spirit." Anna "never left the temple. She worshiped there with fasting and prayer night and day" (Lk 2:37–38). Why? The worn-out priest and the half-crazy prophetess had embraced the notion that God was still working—even in the midst of the muddled mess that surrounded them. So, when God finally showed up, they were able to look past the implausible packaging and recognize a divine Messiah.

Simeon and Anna hadn't merely prayed the prayers of expectation. They fully expected that God would answer their prayers. And God's answer to their prayers was a little boy whose mother would teach him to pray the Amidah long before either the boy or his mother realized that he was the answer to its pleas for a Savior.

Living the Prayers

If the prayer of expectation became a message that we chose to live instead of an obscure relic from the past, what might change?

First of all, the world's definition of "power" wouldn't survive very long. The Jews had asked God, "Cause the descendant of David your servant to flourish, and increase his power." And God did. But God's definition of power didn't require political posturing or military might. God's definition of power entailed meekness, humility, and humiliation—the meekness of an infant, the humility of a carpenter, and the humiliation of a cross. In *The Hungering Dark*, Frederick Buechner reminds us how God came to earth:

He came in such a way that we can always turn him down, as we could crack the baby's skull like an eggshell or nail him up when he gets too big for that. God comes to us in the hungry man that we do not have to feed, comes to us in the lonely man we do not have to comfort, comes to us in all the desperate human need of people everywhere that we are always free to turn our backs upon.[11]

Yet the people of God persist in defining God's presence in terms of human power. You don't believe me? Suppose one of your friends said, "See that person? The power of God is really with her." What sort of person would you expect to see? A newlywed teenager with a hungry baby at her breast and a worried husband at her side? I doubt it. And yet, that's precisely the sort of person who carried the answer to the prayers of expectation into the court-yard of the temple. In the words of the Blessed Virgin Mary, "God has looked favorably on the powerlessness of his servant!... He has pulled the powerful from their thrones and exalted those who had no power!" (Lk 1:48, 52). It's insanity—but it's holy insanity. Best of all, it's the truth.

The Promise of Holy Insanity

God loves to reveal his presence among his people. But he has a penchant for revealing his power through the least likely path-ways—through humility and simplicity, powerlessness and humil-iation. And yet, when we are willing to wait and to watch for God's glory amid the powerlessness of his people, we eventually find our-selves praying with Simeon, "My eyes have seen your salvation in the very places where the world sees only weakness."

Who knows? The reeking alcoholic who barely made it down the aisle to shake the pastor's hand may end up leading your church's recovery program. That new church member who cackles constantly? She may be the greatest prayer warrior in your entire congregation. The junior-high kid who is struggling with the notion of deodorant? Could be he'll become a youth minister. And you? If God can come to earth as a little screecher in the Bethlehem nursery, I'm sure he can do something with you, too.

That's the promise of holy insanity.

————A MEDITATION————

Master,
    my eyes have seen your salvation.
        It doesn't make sense,
           but it works.
Yet sometimes I still catch myself
    expecting you to reveal yourself
        in ways that make sense to me…
    expecting you to save
        the people that *I* would save…
    expecting salvation to occur
        on my terms.
I forget that it's "*your* salvation"—
    not mine.
I have a hard time
    waiting for
        watching for
           longing for
    your salvation…
        your revelation…
           your way of doing things.
My plans make so much more sense,
    but they fall apart so quickly.
Your plans take so long
    and seem so strange
        and so weak,
           but they last forever.
    Help me to watch
        and to wait
           for you.
Amen.

——THE PRAYERS OF BLESSING——

You are blessed, Adonai our God, the king of the universe, he who brings forth bread from the earth.

Traditional Jewish prayer

You are blessed, Adonai, our God—he who has loved us with great love and comforted us with overflowing compassions. You are blessed, Adonai—he who lovingly chose Israel as his people.... You are blessed, Adonai our God. His word unto us is true and firm, forever and ever, unto all generations. You are blessed, Adonai—he who has redeemed Israel. Amen.

Blessings spoken before and after the Shema,
the Jewish confession of faith

The Lord bless you and keep you; the Lord make his face to shine upon you, and be generous to you; the Lord lift up his countenance upon you, and give you peace.

NUMBERS 6:24-26, NRSV

CHAPTER TWO

The God Who Risks:
The Prayers of Blessing

John Bar-Zechariah rubbed his eyes and peered over Joseph's sleeping form. Jesus' space on the floor was already empty, his bedding piled against the wall. John quickly rolled his mat and tiptoed out of the guest room. As he slipped outside, three trumpet blasts pierced the cool, spring air. The daily lots had been cast in the temple. The priests were preparing to offer the morning sacrifices and burn the incense. Within minutes, the scents of seared flesh and incense would saturate the eastern half of the Holy City.

John searched the walled courtyard behind the house before glancing toward the roof. There, he saw his cousin sitting on the edge of the house, watching the sun peek over the Mount of Olives. John scrambled up the steps and flopped beside Jesus.

"What are—?" John began.

"Sssshhh! Listen."

Jangling timbrels and chanting voices resonated from the temple courts. The Levites were singing the praise psalms, the *hallel*,[1] just as they did every morning. John was still trying to decipher which portion they were chanting when Jesus began to recite the words with them:

"The stone that the builders rejected has become the chief cornerstone. This is the doing of *Adonai*; it is marvelous in our sight.

This is the day that the Lord has made. Let us rejoice and exult in it! Oh Lord, deliver us! Oh Lord, let us prosper! May the one who enters be blessed in the name of *Adonai*; We bless you from the House of *Adonai*. *Adonai* is God. He has given—"

"John, Jesus!"

Joseph's voice interrupted the recitation. The cousins clambered down the stairs and into the guest room. Elizabeth, Mary, and the younger children were already gone. Zechariah still lay in the corner of the guest room, snoring loudly. Last night he had told them the story about the messenger who had appeared in the temple to announce John's birth. He told the same story every year when the family gathered here, in the ancestral home of Zechariah's family, for the Passover and the Feast of Unleavened Bread. After hearing it for twelve years, Jesus was quite certain that he remembered the story better than Zechariah. This afternoon every priest, even aged Zechariah, would gather at the temple to offer nearly six hundred thousand Passover lambs—one for each Jewish family that made the pilgrimage to Jerusalem.

When James, little Joseph, and Simon returned with Elizabeth and Mary, Jesus and John followed Joseph behind the house. As they clustered around the dung pit, Joseph told Jesus, "My son, now you are old enough to take the responsibility for keeping the covenant and the commandments. Today, you will speak the blessings and recite the *Shema*. Today you will put on the *tallith* and the *tefillin*.[2] Today we will enter the Court of Israel together to offer the sacrifices. For today, you begin to take the yoke of the Torah upon yourself."[3]

Zechariah hobbled around a bush to join Jesus, Joseph, and John, and intoned in a gravelly voice, "Embrace the Torah with joy, Jesus. It is your life. Its commandments are not too hard or too far away. No, the word is in your mouth and in your heart for you to obey. The Torah is like a well-made yoke upon an ox's shoulders—it brings pain only when the ox struggles against it. If you obey its precepts, the yoke of the Torah will be easy, my son, and the burden will be light."[4]

The twelve-year-old Jesus and his cousin scraped some dirt into the dung pit before turning toward the massive jars that stood beside the house. Jesus gasped as he plunged his hands into one of the jars. The water of purification always seemed as frigid as the snow on Mount Hermon. He scrubbed each of his palms with the opposite fist until Joseph nodded to him. Jesus nodded silently, pondering his great-uncle's words. He drew a deep breath and spoke the blessing: "You are blessed, *Adonai* our God, the king of the universe, he who has sanctified us according to his commandments and commanded us concerning the washing of hands. Amen."

Joseph and Jesus, Zechariah and John, went back in the house and joined the women and children on a woven mat on the floor. Mary had filled two bowls with dried figs and clumps of curds. Conversation, laughter, and memories of Passovers past swelled within the little circle—until Zechariah raised his quavering hands.

Even James and little Joseph hushed as the elder spoke: "Last Passover, my son, John, the child of my old age, took upon himself the responsibility to keep the covenant. This Passover, Jesus begins to prepare himself to become a son of the commandments. Today, he will speak the blessings and the Shema."

Jesus looked downward and recited the blessing for the food, "You are blessed, *Adonai* our God, the king of the universe, he who brings forth bread from the earth." Everyone in the room—except baby Simon, who lay in his mother's arms, nursing noisily—murmured in unison, "Amen."

As he spoke, Mary gazed into her oldest son's dark, brooding eyes. He looked so normal, so ... ordinary. Yet she, more than anyone else, knew that Jesus had never been ordinary. His penetrating questions still unnerved her. The uncertainty of his future terrified her. "A sword will pierce your own heart," the old priest had told her years earlier, and she sensed the twist of the sword again as she searched those eyes and wondered what this child would become.

Jesus' voice disrupted her thoughts. He was speaking the blessings that preceded the Shema: "You are blessed, *Adonai,* our God—he who has loved us with great love and comforted us with overflowing compassion. You are blessed, *Adonai*—he who lovingly chose Israel as his people." When Jesus began to recite the Shema, Mary softly murmured the words in unison with him:

"Hear, oh Israel! *Adonai* is our God, *Adonai* alone. You will love *Adonai* your God with all your heart and with all your soul and with all your might. Take to heart these instructions which I give to you this day. Impress them on your children. Recite them when you stay at home and are away, when you lie down and when you get up. Impress my words upon your heart. Bind them as a sign on your hand and let them serve as a symbol on your forehead, and teach them to your children, reciting them when you stay at home and when you are away, when you lie down and when you get up. Inscribe them on the doorposts of your house and on your gates—so that you and your children may endure, in the land that *Adonai* swore to your fathers to assign to them, as long as there is a heaven over the earth."

Jesus paused before speaking the blessing that marked the end of the Shema: "You are blessed, *Adonai* our God. His word unto us is true and firm, forever and ever, unto all generations. You are blessed, *Adonai*—he who has redeemed Israel. Amen."[5]

When Jesus finished reciting the blessing, no one echoed the "amen." Utter silence filled the guest room. Jesus had not recited the words of the Shema as if he believed them to be true. He had spoken them as if he *knew* they were true, as if the words did not flow from the ancient scrolls but from his own heart. And the sword wrenched within Mary again as she ached to understand this child whom she loved as her own but who never truly seemed to belong to her.

Finally, the voice of Zechariah shattered the silence. "Son of Mary." He placed his hand on Jesus' shoulder and spoke the priestly blessing: "May *Adonai* bless you and protect you! May *Adonai* deal kindly and graciously with you! May *Adonai* bestow his favor upon you and grant you peace! Amen."

Why Blessed?

The prayer, "You are blessed,[6] *Adonai*," punctuated every part of the ancient Jews' lives. Before they ate, after they ate, when they plunged their hands into the waters of purification, when they saw a rainbow, when they lit the Sabbath candles, when they wrapped themselves in their prayer shawls, when they ended their celebrations of the Sabbath, before and after they recited their central confession of faith—the Shema—they prayed, "You are blessed, *Adonai*."[7]

Moreover, the word "blessed" reverberated throughout the life of Jesus. When his mother showed up on Elizabeth's front porch, Elizabeth cried, "Blessed are you among women, and blessed is the fruit of your womb!" When Simon Peter stumbled into a recognition of his teacher's identity, Jesus declared, "Blessed are you, Simon Bar-Jonah!" When clusters of squirming rug-rats clamored to be cuddled by the miracle worker from Nazareth, Jesus "gathered them into his arms ... and blessed them." On the night of his betrayal, Jesus "took bread, blessed, and broke it." His final earthly act was to bless the women and men who stuck around long enough to see him return to his Father. While he was blessing them, his Father welcomed him home (see Mt 14:19; 16:17; Mk 10:16; Lk 1:42–45; 24:30, 51).

What did the Jews mean when they prayed "You are blessed"? The root of the Hebrew word for "blessed," *barukh,* means "to bow." The noun form means "knee," as in "bow the knee." So if I truly bless someone, I do not merely wish him well; I submit to him. I give myself to him. In short, I become vulnerable.

When the Jews sang "Bless the Lord, oh my soul," they admitted that they were bound not only to offer their praises to God but also to offer themselves.[8] When the Israelites prayed "Blessed be the Lord," or "You are blessed, oh Lord," they acknowledged something even greater—they recognized God's desire to give himself to them. Through those words, the Jews confessed that their God was willing to become vulnerable for the sake of his people.

The Vulnerability of Blessedness

God's longing to give himself to humanity is as ancient as the Garden of Eden. In the garden, he refused to keep the joy of creating new life to himself—on Adam and Eve's wedding night, "God blessed them and said, 'Be fruitful and multiply, and fill the earth'" (Gn 1:28). Later, he refused to retain the satisfaction of ownership for himself—he blessed a petulant band of former pyramid-builders with a land that flowed with milk and honey (see Dt 6:15; 28:3–6). In the Incarnation, he even refused to keep heaven to himself—he came to earth and risked our rejection to populate heaven with the likes of you and me. In the words of the Nicene Creed, "For us and for our salvation, he came down."

And oh, how he "came down"! He encased his deity in a microscopic embryo that grew for nine months beneath the heart of a peasant girl. "His last true comfort was that final moment before slipping from his mother's womb. Then, a borrowed feeding trough met him, and the story of his pain began."[9] He had emerged in an insignificant corner of the Roman Empire as a baby who couldn't speak or eat solid food or control his bladder.[10] God endured *puberty*, for heaven's sake! His hometown was in the province of Galilee. "As Cajun Country is to New Orleans and Kerry is to Dublin, the Galilean hills were the ultimate Boonies, the archetypical setting for all of arch Jerusalem's hayseed jokes."[11]

Through his incarnation in Jesus Christ, God embraced the deepest degree of vulnerability. God blessed his creation in the most indisputable way. And at the intersection of two blood-soaked beams of wood, the full meaning of blessedness became painfully clear. For on the cross, the omnipotent Creator submitted to the pain and misery of his shattered world.

The story of God's love affair with humanity is a constant cycle of his people forgetting, remembering, then recovering what it means to bless and to be blessed. Perhaps that's why the Jews began and ended their recitations of the Shema by recognizing the blessedness of God: "You are blessed, *Adonai* our God—he who has loved us with great love and comforted us with overflowing compassion. You are blessed, *Adonai*—he who lovingly chose Israel as his people.... You are blessed, *Adonai*—he who has redeemed Israel."

Blessings and Favors

Still, the Jews consistently forgot the meaning of blessedness and confused *blessings* with *favors*—and more often than we would like to admit, so do we. Pay close attention to the difference: A favor is a cheap, short-lived present, usually given out of duty (think of a "party favor"). A blessing, on the other hand, is a conscious choice to open myself to the possibility of pain and rejection. I can do a favor for someone and risk nothing. Not so when I bless someone. By commanding the Israelites to repeat the words, "May the Lord bless you," the living God was not only demonstrating his good favor toward them. He was also declaring that he had chosen to become vulnerable. He was expressing his willingness to risk rejection at the hands of his own people.

Yet beneath our comfortable cloaks of creeds and curricula and confessions of faith, I suspect that most of us still believe that God operates according to the same rules as our world, a system in which we give favors to earn favors. Like a spoiled child in a toy store, we assume that if we have done our chores ("I read through the Bible again this year!") and if we ask politely ("I pray this in Jesus' name"), our Father will give us the favors that we want. In the process, we miss completely what it means to bless and to be blessed.

When we believe that God interacts with humanity according to a system of favors, one of two things happens: Some persons, like the Pharisees of the first century, come to believe that they can do enough favors to earn God's favor. They are fooling themselves. Others recognize that they can never do enough favors to earn God's favor, but they still run themselves ragged trying. These Christians attend every committee meeting, teach every class, and fix every leaky faucet in the church building. They are the women and men who do so many favors for God's people that they never learn to receive and rejoice in God's blessings. They work to earn a love they already possess and are terrified of forfeiting a love they can never lose.

There is, however, another group of people, those whom Jesus called the "poor in spirit." These folk recognize that they have nothing to offer God. More importantly, they realize that what God craves from us is not a statistical increase in our number of good deeds. What he wants is *us,* prepared to be transformed and stripped of our pitiful attempts to impress him.

Even greater, what God wants to give to us is not a string of cosmic party favors—a bit more prestige in one part of our lives, fewer problems in another. God commanded his people to speak the words, "The LORD bless you and keep you," because he wanted to give his children the gift of himself. Blessedness is not about receiving things; it is about receiving God. To receive the blessing of God's presence is to rejoice in God not because he does favors for us but because he has shared his own, sacred identity with us.

Becoming the Blessing

There's a catch when it comes to receiving God's blessing, though: "I will bless you," God informed Abraham, "so that you will be a blessing" (Gn 12:2). If I have truly received God's blessing, I must become the blessing of God to the people around me—and becoming a blessing isn't easy. Simon Peter described the blessed life in this way: "Never repay evil for evil or abuse for abuse. Instead, repay with a blessing. It is for this that you were called, that you might inherit a blessing" (1 Pt 3:9). When I become the blessing of God, I respond to every person and every event in my life according to a set of values that differs radically from the world around me.

I refuse to allow the opinions of others to erode my joy, because my Father has given himself to me and he is the Source of Joy.

I refuse to seek revenge, because my Father has given himself to me and he is the judge of the universe.

I refuse to keep track of others' faults, because my Father has refused to keep track of mine.

If I become this sort of person, the bad news is that I can end up hurt. The good news is that I no longer care where I end up, because I have found my joy and value not in myself or in my circumstances but in my God.

It isn't easy to live a life of blessedness. Frankly, becoming the blessing of God can hurt ... deeply. When I become God's blessing, I am forced to recognize the full breadth of my own selfishness. How often have I refused to say to a church member who has wronged me, "If I have offended you, please forgive me"? How often have I longed to weep while praying with a teen—but fought the tears until my temples throbbed rather than risk the appearance of being weak? How often have I sat piously in my pew during a worship service while my mind flitted from one self-centered fantasy to another?

To refuse to hold a grudge against the church member was a favor—to ask for forgiveness would have been a blessing. To pray with the youth was a favor—to weep over her would have been a blessing. To gather with God's people was a favor—to submit my entire being to God would have been a blessing. This definition of blessedness will never achieve the cultural popularity that contemporary Christians seem to crave—but, then again, neither did Jesus Christ.

Necessary, But Not Easy

Let's be honest: The life of blessing is embarrassing, offensive, and difficult. If we call ourselves followers of Jesus Christ, it is also absolutely necessary. Brennan Manning puts it this way:

The love of our God isn't dignified at all, and apparently that's the way He expects our love to be. Not only does He require that we accept His inexplicable, embarrassing kind of love, but once we've accepted it, He expects us to behave the same way with others. I suppose I could live, if I had to, with a God whose love for us is embarrassing, but the thought that I've got to act that way with other people—that's a bit too much to swallow.[12]

Jesus once commented, "Blessed is the one who takes no offense at me"—literally, "Blessed is the one who is not scandalized by me" (Lk 7:23). Allow me to paraphrase his words: "Blessed are the ones who are not embarrassed by my undignified, uncomfortable, untamed love. They are the ones who truly love me. They are the ones who will carry my love beyond human borders to people who are glutted with favors and yet starved for blessings. They are the ones who understand what it means to pray, 'You are blessed, *Adonai* our God, the king of the universe.'" From the world's perspective, that's the love of a loser. From God's perspective, it's the only love worth giving one's life to achieve.

——A MEDITATION——

Blessed be the Lord!
Blessed be the Servant-King!
Blessed be the Vulnerable God!

It's so easy to envision you as a regal ruler,
   exalted upon your throne.
Or as a mighty warrior,
   ready to fight for your people.
Or as the sovereign spirit,
   turning nothingness into a living cosmos.

It's not so easy to envision you on your knees—
   not exalted but on your knees—
      on your knees
         at my service,
         at my disposal.
It's hard to accept the reality,
   and the humility,
      of a God
         who chooses to be a blessing,
         who chooses to be vulnerable.

And it's even harder to humble myself.
I don't mind bowing to some people ...
   kind people,
      clean people,
         righteous people.
But to bless anyone...

the unkind

("Like it was my fault he was having a bad day!"),

the unclean

("But, Lord, she hasn't taken a bath in months!

And, well ... I don't think her elevator stops

on all the floors"),

the unrighteous

("OK, here's where I draw the line:

It's his fault that he has AIDS

and I've got to think about my family's health.

No, I will not serve...

Yes, yes—I know ... *anyone*").

Lord, why does it have to be so difficult?
I like to be selective in my service.

Let me serve like you served—
  you weren't selective.
If you had been, you would never have selected me.
    Amen.[13]

——The Wedding Blessings——

You are blessed, *Adonai* our God, king of the universe, he who created the fruit of the vine!

You are blessed, *Adonai* our God, king of the universe, he who created all things for his glory!

You are blessed, *Adonai* our God, king of the universe, he who created humanity!

You are blessed, *Adonai* our God, king of the universe, he who created humanity in his own image, for creating them as mates so that they too may create life!

You are blessed, *Adonai* our God, king of the universe, he who makes the groom and bride rejoice in each other—may he give gladness to them as he gave gladness to his creatures in the Garden of Eden!

You are blessed, *Adonai* our God, king of the universe, the Source of Joy and Gladness!

You are blessed, *Adonai* our God, king of the universe, he who causes the groom to rejoice in the bride! Amen.

Sheva B'rakhot,
the Jewish wedding blessings

CHAPTER THREE

The Source of Joy:
The Wedding Blessings

The Roman Empire was as peaceful as it ever had been. Emperor Tiberius had ruled his father's sprawling domain for fifteen years. He was an able administrator who according to the latest gossip had a peculiar proclivity for prepubescent boys. The only urgent message on his desk concerned the collapse of a shoddily built theater in Fidenae. Nearly thirty thousand Romans had perished when the foundation suddenly failed.

Judea's provincial governor—a new appointee named Pilate—had recently sent a squad of soldiers to the edge of the wilderness to check out a long-haired revolutionary who was prophesying about a new king. When they returned to Pilate's quarters, the soldiers were still guffawing. The self-proclaimed prophet smelled like a dead camel and looked worse. And he had the audacity to tell the soldiers to stop plundering people's property![1] How else could they make ends meet? Not on the paltry payments the Senate allotted them!

Few people in the province of Galilee cared about Fidenae's building code or Pilate's soldiers or what happened in Tiberius' bedchambers on the isle of Capri. Most Galileans simply wanted every part of their lives to be left alone—especially their purses and their religious practices. Unfortunately, the Roman Empire meddled frequently in both. After a handful of skirmishes with Roman troops, the citizens of Galilee had become known as a gang of hot-heads and potential terrorists. The portrayal wasn't completely fair, but it stuck.

Herod Antipas, the tetrarch of Galilee and Perea, had kept a lid on his provinces for three decades. While no one admired Antipas enough to extol him, no one despised him enough to dethrone him. That was probably as much as a professional politician could expect in Galilee. Of course, Antipas didn't strengthen his popularity among the Jews when he swapped his wife for a niece who also happened to be his sister-in-law. His standing in their polls took another nose-dive when he encouraged Gentiles to populate the newly built port city of Tiberias.

But even the relentless shadows of the Roman Empire could not dim the joy that radiated from the Galilean village of Cana one particular evening. Cana was a scattered cluster of houses, draped across a terraced hill about 120 stadia west of Tiberias.[2] In the guest room of one house, women and men reclined on woven mats and cushions. Embroidered tapestries spanned the chamber, forming tents above the friends and family members who had gathered in the newly built home of the *chatan*, the bridegroom. The mingled scents of smoldering lamps, human sweat, and spices soaked the sultry air.

The bride—the *kallah*—and her beloved stood before the *chuppah* and the *cheder*, the lavish canopy draped over one end of the room and the bed the couple would share when the wedding feast ended. The bride's hair, crowned with a circlet of ten silver coins and saturated with myrrh, glistened in the lamplight.[3] The chatan, his shoulders encircled with a garland of flowers, declared, "She is my wife and I am her husband from this day and forever."[4] As the couple washed their hands in the stone water pots used for purification rites, the guests murmured, "Amen."

Nathanael Bar-Tolmai, one of the bridegroom's relatives, lay on a cushion beside the water pots.[5] He was a local boy—likable, but with a reputation for squandering his afternoons beneath the shade trees. His latest circle of friends reclined around him. Yet it wasn't Nathanael who had drawn this band together; the hub of the group was a young carpenter named Jesus. He was a native of Nazareth, a seedy community about seventy-five stadia south of Cana.

The carpenter's mother lay behind her son. Drops of sweat wandered down her forehead, over the deep furrows and past the wisps of gray hair. Her eyes were fixed on the kallah and the chatan, but her thoughts were far from Cana. She wondered if her oldest son would ever embrace a young woman before the cheder and the chuppah. If he did, what sort of woman would she be? He attracted the strangest mix of people. Nathanael and Philip were pious and polite. Simon, Andrew, and Zebedee's sons were rough but still respectable. But then there was that tramp from Magdala! Mary shuddered at the rumors she had heard about why the woman had suddenly left the city of Magdala. Mary wanted her son to be married—but not to a trollop like that, with red henna on her fingernails and balena smeared around her eyes like plaster on the side of a stable! Why, oh why, Mary wondered, does he let *her* hang around him? Who will end up at his side next?

Mary knew why her son attracted such motley folk. It wasn't because he was the life of the party, although he delighted in feasts and enjoyed a good joke as much as anyone else. Nor was it his spontaneity, although he had been known to make friends by walking up to strangers and declaring, "Follow me!" Jesus drew people to him because of the contentment and the gentle strength that flowed from every word he spoke.

Her son's gentleness both captivated and terrified her. After thirty years, the white-robed messenger's words still pierced her heart: "He will reign forever over the house of Jacob. His kingdom will never end!"[6] Had she heard the messenger's words correctly? Jesus was the son of God—that she could never deny. Yet if the motley mob that lounged around him comprised his army, how could he be the Messiah? And if gentleness was his only weapon, how could he become a king?

Mary watched as the groom's father dipped a cup into the jar of wine. He raised the cup above the couple and spoke the *sheva b'rakhot*, the wedding blessings:

"You are blessed, *Adonai* our God, king of the universe, he who created the fruit of the vine!

"You are blessed, *Adonai* our God, king of the universe, he who created all things for his glory!

"You are blessed, *Adonai* our God, king of the universe, he who created humanity!

"You are blessed, *Adonai* our God, king of the universe, he who created humanity in his own image, for creating them as mates so that they too may create life!

"You are blessed, *Adonai* our God, king of the universe, he who makes the groom and bride rejoice in each other—may he give gladness to them as he gave gladness to his creatures in the Garden of Eden!

"You are blessed, *Adonai* our God, king of the universe, the Source of Joy and Gladness!

"You are blessed, *Adonai* our God, king of the universe, he who causes the groom to rejoice in the bride! Amen."[7]

The newlyweds drained the cup, and raucous shouts erupted from Nathanael's circle of friends. The betrothal—that incessant season of waiting—was over. Now it was time for brimming cups of wine, yeasty chunks of bread, smoked slabs of lamb, and endless heaps of grapes and figs. The wedding feast had begun!

The Infinite Emptiness

From the beginning, every human heart has craved infinite delight. A dark, hungry void gnaws at every human being's innermost self. "This infinite emptiness," Blaise Pascal declared, "can only be filled by an infinite and immutable object, that is to say, only by God himself."[8] The church father Augustine of Hippo described the dilemma in this way: "Oh Lord, you made us for yourself, and our heart is restless until it finds its rest in you."[9]

Yet people cannot fathom that their thirst for infinite pleasure is, ultimately, a craving for the creator of pleasure. So they try to quench their thirst with finite pleasures—another beer, another sexual partner, one more degree, one more dollar, a piece of fruit that promises the knowledge of good and evil. The personal compulsions differ, but the core problem remains the same: Few persons truly believe that God is the source of pleasure. They cannot fathom that there are, in the psalmist's words, "pleasures forevermore" within the being of God (Ps 16:11).

Yet each time they celebrated a marriage, the ancient Jews recognized the infinite pleasure of God. At every wedding, the groom's father or a community leader repeated the sheva b'rakhot:

> You are blessed, *Adonai* our God, king of the universe, he who created humanity in his own image, for creating them as mates so that they too may create life!... You are blessed, *Adonai* our God, king of the universe, the Source of Joy and Gladness! You are blessed, *Adonai* our God, king of the universe, he who causes the groom to rejoice in the bride! Amen.

The Jewish wedding blessings explicitly acknowledged that the delight of the intimate relationship between a wife and her husband—perhaps the supreme expression of pleasure on the planet—is rooted in God, "the Source of Joy and Gladness."

If God is "the Source of Joy," it shouldn't surprise us that one of the Hebrew prophets' favorite depictions of God's relationship with his people was the image of a passionate lover seeking the pleasure of his bride.[10] Here's how Ezekiel and Hosea described God's relationship with Israel:

> This is what the Lord says: I watched you grow into womanhood. Your breasts grew firm. Your hair sprouted. You were naked, and I saw that your time for love had arrived. I enfolded you in my cloak, and I entered into a covenant with you by oath. You became mine. I bathed you with water and poured fragrant oils over your body. Now, I will take you away to a deserted place and speak to you tenderly. There you will respond to me like you did in the days when you were young.
>
> from EZEKIEL 16:7–14 and HOSEA 2:14–15, 19

God ... depicted as a groom bathing with his bride and rejoicing in her nakedness? God ... pictured as a husband, whisking away his wife to a secluded love nest where she would respond like a newlywed for whom the experience is fresh and new? God ... the Cosmic Lover, delighting in the pleasure of his people? God ... the Source of Joy? Even though images of God as a passionate lover pervade the pages of Scripture, many contemporary Christians aren't comfortable with such portrayals of God. In the view of many Christians, pleasure may not be sinful, but it certainly isn't sacred. You don't believe me? When was the last time you knelt beside the bed before having sex with your spouse and thanked God for the feast that you are preparing to share?[11]

In essence, that's what is implied by the wedding blessings offered at Jewish weddings such as the one Jesus attended in Cana. To embrace the implications of the wedding blessings is to admit that joy and pleasure are holy. That doesn't mean that every *form* of joy or pleasure is holy. Neither does it allow us to focus our lives on finite pleasures. It does, however, call Christians to rejoice in God's presence by enjoying every ordinary pleasure that he places in our paths.

That means rejoicing in God's presence when I stroke my wife's skin and my heart begins to race; when I snuggle a toddler and savor the sweet scent of his hair; when I look at a sunset; when I am stuck in rush-hour traffic and take a few moments to think about the silvery sparkle of a seventh-grade girl's giggle; when I recognize that God loves the church member who constantly criticizes me and, therefore, I can love him too. To recognize God as the Source of Joy is to embrace every finite experience as a representation of God's infinite joy.

Divine Pleasure Versus Cultural Consumerism

One reason that contemporary Christians have a difficult time viewing God as the Source of Joy is that our culture has attempted to replace authentic pleasure and joy with consumerism. The message of consumerism is simple: Consuming an excess of artificial pleasures can satisfy humanity's hunger for infinite pleasure. Television commercials and newspaper advertisements proclaim this gospel millions of times each day. According to one recent ad, "Whoever said it's better to give than to receive was obviously never on the receiving end of this car.... What more could you hope for?"

Another ad declares, "This holiday, we'd like to encourage excessive drinking. Water, of course.... Indulge. It's a good thing."

The ditties may differ, but the results are the same: If we accept their message, life becomes a frenzied struggle for *more* as we try to fill our infinite emptiness with an excess of finite pleasures. The drunk tries to cure his hangover with another beer. The middle-aged man desperately combs the Internet for a more alluring picture of a more perfect model in a more explicit pose. The first-grader wails in the aisle of Wal-Mart, "If I only get this one, I'll never ask for another toy again!" The teen glances across the grandeur of the Painted Desert and declares with disgust, "We came all the way out here to see dirt, rocks, and dead trees?"—and then immerses himself in the lifeless pixels prancing across the face of a handheld game. Adults have four-car garages attached to households of two, television sets in every room of the house, closets that bulge with clothes we never wear, and waistlines that bulge because of calories we never needed. In a consumerist culture

> we no longer catch our breath at the sight of a rainbow or the scent of a rose, as we once did.... We no longer run our fingers through water, no longer shout at the stars, or make faces at the moon.... Certainly, the new can amaze us: a space shuttle, the latest computer game, the softest diaper. Till tomorrow, till the new becomes old, till yesterday's wonder is discarded or taken for granted.[12]

A recent article in *USA Today* included this unwitting indictment of consumerism:

We buy, buy, buy, hoping to fill that empty, yearning hole in our soul. And as we rack up more debt, we buy possessions in a useless attempt to comfort ourselves.... Every time I add something to my pile, I feel a whoosh of pleasure, like a fire-work going off. And for a moment, everything's all right. But then, gradually, the light and sparkles disappear, and I'm left with cold, dark blackness again. So I look around feverishly for something else.... But the whooshes are getting shorter and shorter each time. Why won't the pleasures stay? Why don't I feel happier?[13]

The solution is not simply choosing to be satisfied with what we have—although that would be a good place to start! We must embrace the wisdom found in the ancient Jewish wedding bless-ings—we must recognize God as "the Source of Gladness and Joy" and allow him to satisfy our deepest longings. When we do, we begin to discover infinite joy in the ordinary events of our lives— "in a glance or a touch or a song, in a field of corn or a friend who cares, in a moon or an amoeba, in a lifeless loaf suddenly become the body of Christ."[14]

What Does God Desire?
Unfortunately, the typical person's relationship with God functions more like an impersonal business transaction than a passionate evening with one's spouse. A high-pressure sales pitch brings peo-ple down the aisle to sign a contract. Some congregations call the contract "An Application for Church Membership." Others use less formal clichés—"The Four Spiritual Laws" and "Admit, Believe, Confess." The contract grants Jesus Christ more or less complete control of their lives and requires that they meet with

him for occasional updates. In return, God gives them everlasting life. This system would be satisfactory except for a single damning difficulty: No contract can compel what God desires—our passionate, joyous love. God is, in the words of the fourteenth-century mystic Catherine of Siena, "*pazzo d'amore, ebro d'amore*"[15]—"impassioned and intoxicated with love."

The central command of Scripture is, "Love the Lord your God with all your heart, and with all your soul, and with all your mind, and with all your strength" (Mk 12:30). If I love my wife, I will not merely be faithful to her; I will delight in her with passion and joy. The author of the Proverbs explicitly ordered his son, "Find joy in the wife of your youth.... Let her breasts satisfy you at all times. Be infatuated with love of her always" (Prv 5:18-19). Likewise, if I truly love God, I will passionately rejoice in him. Simon Peter wrote, "Although you have never seen Jesus, you love him. Although you cannot see him now, you trust in him and rejoice in him with a glorious joy that words cannot describe" (1 Pt 1:8). The Westminster Catechism echoes the message of Scripture: "The chief end of man is to glorify God and *enjoy him forever*." God's intent for humanity is infinite pleasure and joy.

When God Popped the Cork

When we read the account of the wedding at Cana, it's easy to miss that point. The commentaries on the text offer plenty of facts and conjectures about first-century Jewish weddings: Every guest brought gifts of food and wine. The feasts frequently lasted a full week. It was shameful if the food or wine ran out during the feast. Perhaps Mary informed Jesus that the wine was gone because he had not contributed anything to the feast. Perhaps God had revealed to the Blessed Virgin that it was time for Jesus to begin his earthly ministry.

In the midst of these details and speculations, we can miss the central point of the text: *In the person of Jesus Christ, the eternal pleasure of God erupted in the midst of the counterfeit pleasures of a fallen world.* His earthly ministry began at an event permeated with implications of pleasure. His first miracle was to transform the plain water of a cultural ritual into an exquisite drink of exhilaration and joy.[16] The earthly ministry of Jesus Christ began with these words ringing in his ears: "You are blessed, *Adonai* our God, king of the universe, he who created the fruit of the vine!... You are blessed, *Adonai* our God, king of the universe, the Source of Joy and Gladness!... You are blessed, *Adonai* our God, king of the universe, he who causes the groom to rejoice in the bride!" How, then, can our relationship with God be anything less than a relationship rooted in infinite joy?

Let's put the point in more picturesque terms: In Jesus Christ, God popped the cork on the vintage wine he had stashed in his cellar at the dawn of time. Occasionally God had allowed the ancient prophets to sip this wine, but it was too strong for them. They ended up eating bugs for breakfast, choking down scrolls for dinner, dreaming about creatures with four faces, and bellowing about an unearthly burning in their bones (see Jer 20:9; Ez 1:1-21; 3:1–3; Mt 3:4). They could not manipulate the pleasure of God into a package that fit their cultural and political values. Perhaps that's why so many Israelites settled for the pure but predictable water of the Law. The pleasure of God is like a magnum bottle of the finest Merlot—extravagant, unpredictable, overwhelming, and costly.

When God's people live the sheva b'rakhot—when they embrace God as "the Source of Joy and Gladness"—nothing can remain the same. Waiting on others is no longer a chore—to serve the Body of Christ is to delight in our Beloved. The Lord's Supper is no longer a stale ritual in which the pastor fumbles with crumbled bits of crackers and thimble-sized cups of grape juice. It is a candlelight dinner with the love of our lives. The Bible is no longer a series of static principles that we always accept and occasionally obey. It is a precious love letter that gives us a glimpse of our Lover's deepest hopes and dreams.

Such an understanding of God transforms our prayers from a series of demands, aimed at making our lives easier, into an intimate conversation with our Beloved. Prayer becomes like slipping into a soothing tub of hot water and letting God's love wash over us and enfold us. Through prayer, we enter the inner chamber of our Beloved. He embraces us, and we explore each other with hunger and passion. We entwine our lives with the life of our Savior, he enters the inmost part of our being, and we hear him gently whisper, "I'm wild about you."

Living in Abandonment

How can we learn to live the sheva b'rakhot? How do we embrace God as "the Source of Joy and Gladness"? I wish that I could supply you with a seven-step plan, guaranteed to immerse your life in the joy of God. I can't. I'm still struggling to finish the first step (which is, I suspect, the only step—but it's a long, *long* step).

The first step is total abandonment to the desire to unite my life with Jesus Christ. In the words of the apostle Paul, "I forget what lies behind, and ... I press on toward the goal for the prize of the upward call of God in Christ Jesus" (Phil 3:13-14). I don't mean that we should abandon the pleasures of this life. Quite the opposite! When I live in abandonment, every part of my life *becomes* pleasurable because I embrace every moment as an opportunity to unite my life with "the Source of Joy and Gladness." In the words of Brennan Manning,

> Jesus slept. I can unite my sleep with his. I'm having a rollicking good time at a Cajun barbecue in New Orleans. I shout with them, *"Laissez les bon temps rouler!"* Let the good times roll, and connect with Jesus who multiplied the wine at Cana to keep the party going.... Concretely, abandonment consists in seeing the will of God in all the people, events, and circumstances present to you. If God tears up your beautiful game plan and leads you into a valley instead of onto a mountaintop, it is because he wants you to discover *his* plan, which is more beautiful than anything you or I could have dreamed up.[17]

When I live in abandonment, I do not own my possessions. I recognize that I am only the temporary trustee of a tiny handful of God's possessions. That's why Jesus commanded his disciples, "Give to everyone who begs from you! Do not refuse anyone who wants to borrow from you! If someone takes away your possessions, don't ask for them back" (Mt 5:42; Lk 6:30). Let me paraphrase his words: "Don't hesitate to let others use your belongings. If some of your possessions never find their way home, who cares? They belonged to God anyway. If God decides that he needs them, he can find them without your help." That is living in abandonment.

To live in abandonment is to become *free*—free to give away anything that we possess; free to ignore the commercials that correlate our happiness with our buying habits; free to rejoice in the hints of our Savior's presence in every part of our lives; free to gaze into the heavens, to feel the gentle caress of God, and to whisper into the wind, "My whole being rejoices in God my Savior" (Is 61:10). Only then have we experienced authentic joy. Only then can we be satisfied. For only then have we embraced the sweeping implications of the simple prayer, "You are blessed, *Adonai* our God, the king of the universe, the Source of Joy and Gladness."

——A Meditation——

My Lord, my Lover, the Source of my Joy,
Let me rejoice in you.
Let me delight in your creation,
  in sun and surf,
  in snow and star,
  in blue marlin and robin redbreast,
  in the persons whom I love to love,
      in the persons whom I would prefer not to love,
      in the pleasure of your presence within me.
Let me live a life of abandonment—
a life in which I let go of everything,
  everything that shackles me to yesterday,
  everything that imprisons me in my small self today,
  everything that terrifies me
      with the uncertainty of tomorrow,
          everything except you.
Let me find my pleasure in you—
  because then (and only then) am I free.
      Please, let me be free.
Amen.[18]

II.

KNOWING THE GOD WHOSE GIFTS GO BEYOND OUR EXPECTATIONS

The disciples expected the king of the Israelites—
    what they got was a God
            who wanted Gentiles in his kingdom too.
The disciples expected to become warriors—
        Jesus told them to become the children
            of his Abba instead.
The disciples expected Lazarus
to erupt from his tomb at the end of time—
        four days after he died,
                they had dinner with him.
In the end, the disciples received
  nothing they expected,
        very little they wanted,
            and everything they needed.
Still today,
        that tends to be the way
            God answers prayer.

——THE AMIDAH——

You are blessed, *Adonai* our God, the God of our ancestors, the God of Abraham, the God of Isaac, the God of Jacob.

You are blessed, *Adonai* our God, a great, mighty, and awesome God, the Highest God, the Creator of heaven and earth, our Shield, and the Shield of our ancestors, our confidence in every generation. You are blessed, *Adonai*, the Shield of Abraham! You are strong. You humble the proud, and you judge the merciless. You live forever, and you raise the dead. You cause the wind to blow, and you send the dew. You sustain the living, and you give life to the dead. In the twinkling of an eye, you cause salvation to arise for us. You are blessed, *Adonai*—you who give life to the dead!

Accept us, *Adonai* our God! Dwell in Zion!...

You are blessed, *Adonai*! We serve you in reverent fear. We thank you, *Adonai*, our God and the God of our ancestors, for all good things, for your steadfast love, and for the mercy with which you dealt with us and with our ancestors. When our feet slipped, your steadfast love kept us from falling.

You are blessed, *Adonai*! It is good to thank you! Speedily cause the descendant of David your servant to flourish, and increase his power by your salvation, for we hope for your salvation every day. Amen.[1]

The *Amidah*,
traditional Jewish prayer prayed during the synagogue service

CHAPTER FOUR

God's Unwelcome Answer:
The *Amidah*

The double-blast of the trumpet echoed again over the Galilean hills before escaping across the Plain of Esdraelon. The sun, setting on the other side of Mount Carmel, cast a shadow across the cluster of buildings nestled in the breast of Mount Tabor. On the flat roof of one house the *chazan*, the ruler of the synagogue, laid aside his trumpet and watched the residents of Nazareth scurry toward the synagogue.[2] This Sabbath, the building would be full. Jesus of Nazareth had returned home, and everyone hoped to see a miracle.[3]

The Nazarenes were not excited because they loved the son of Joseph—far from it. Most of them had ignored him when he had lived among them. They were excited because the crowds from Cana and Capernaum had claimed that Jesus could heal the sick, that he spoke like a prophet, that his teachings were plain yet powerful. At first, the Nazarenes had scoffed and snorted—*Jesus, a prophet? Hah! A donkey would be more likely to proclaim the message of God than Jesus Bar-Joseph.* Still, the gossip continued to reach Nazareth. A prophet ... a healer ... perhaps the Messiah! Now, Jesus Bar-Joseph had returned to his hometown. This Sabbath, he would serve as the *sheliach tsibbur*, the teacher of the congregation, in the synagogue of Nazareth, and everyone hoped to see a miracle.

Within the synagogue, a circle of lamps chased away the darkness around the *tebhah*, the chest where the sacred scrolls rested, wrapped in linen. The leaders of the synagogue sat in the seats of honor beside the sacred chest.[4] As the citizens of Nazareth entered the synagogue, they glanced eagerly at the seats of honor—but Jesus was not there. Their eyes desperately scanned the congregation. Where was he? Ah! There—among the common people.... Silent.... Head covered and bowed. Jesus of Nazareth.

At last, the leader of the synagogue stood and summoned Jesus. A strained silence swept the congregation as he ascended the platform and stood behind the lectern. A firm voice filled the room with the invocation:

"You are blessed, *Adonai*, the ruler of the world. You formed light, and you created darkness. You formed peace, and you created all things. In your mercy, you give light to the earth and to everyone who lives on the earth. In your goodness, you renew your creation daily. You are blessed, *Adonai* our God, for the glory of his works! You are blessed, *Adonai* our God, for the lights—he made them for his praise! You are blessed, *Adonai* our God—it was he who formed the light!

"You have loved us with great love, *Adonai* our God. You have comforted us with overflowing compassion, our Father and our King. Have mercy on us and teach us, for the sake of our ancestors who trusted in you and received from you the laws of life. Open our eyes to your law. Cause our hearts to cling to your commandments. Unite our hearts to love and fear your name. Then, we will never be put to shame. For you are a God who creates salvation! You have chosen us from all nations and languages! Truly, you have drawn us close to your name so that we can lovingly praise you in your Oneness. You are blessed, *Adonai*, you who lovingly chose Israel as his people!"[5]

Jesus then recited the Shema, turned toward the tebhah, and knelt. The congregation joined him as he began to repeat the Amidah:

"You are blessed, *Adonai* our God, the God of our ancestors, the God of Abraham, the God of Isaac, the God of Jacob.

"You are blessed, *Adonai* our God, a great, mighty, and awesome God, the Highest God, the Creator of heaven and earth, our Shield, and the Shield of our ancestors, our confidence in every generation. You are blessed, *Adonai*, the Shield of Abraham! You are strong. You humble the proud, and you judge the merciless. You live forever, and you raise the dead. You cause the wind to blow, and you send the dew. You sustain the living, and you give life to the dead. In the twinkling of an eye, you cause salvation to arise for us. You are blessed, *Adonai*—you who give life to the dead!

"Accept us, *Adonai* our God! Dwell in Zion!...

"You are blessed, *Adonai!* We serve you in reverent fear. We thank you, *Adonai*, our God and the God of our ancestors, for all good things, for your steadfast love, and for the mercy with which you dealt with us and with our ancestors. When our feet slipped, your steadfast love kept us from falling.

"You are blessed, *Adonai!* It is good to thank you! Speedily cause the descendant of David your servant to flourish, and increase his power by your salvation, for we hope for your salvation every day. Amen."

The synagogue ruler removed the Torah scroll from the tebhah. He unwound the blue and crimson cloths, ascended the platform, and unrolled the sacred scroll. The first leader of the synagogue read a portion from the Torah, then the second, and the third. With each reading, the crowd grew more restless. After the readings from the Torah, Jesus would begin to teach. Finally, after the seventh reading, the chazan nodded to Jesus.

Jesus accepted the scroll of Isaiah. As he ascended the platform, Jesus stopped and surveyed the congregation, packed into the familiar, wooden benches, standing in the dim corners of the lamp-lit room, peering through the windows—the women, jammed together, near the back of the room. The only sound in the synagogue was a faint rustling as Jesus unrolled the scroll and deliberately skimmed the planate columns of sacred text. At last, he began to read, speaking as if he knew the words by heart, paraphrasing the Hebrew text into Aramaic:

"The Spirit of *Adonai* is on me, because he has anointed me. He has sent me to proclaim good news to the poor, to announce freedom to the captives and restoration of sight to the blind, to free the broken, and to proclaim the year acceptable to *Adonai*."[6]

Jesus waited as the congregation absorbed the final echoes of the messianic prophecy. He handed the scroll to the chazan and lowered himself into the chair beside the lectern. Few people could escape the irony—the carpenter's son, sitting in the seat of the teacher. Jesus leaned forward, squinting slightly in the fading light. His eyes seemed to pierce each person's deepest ambitions and plumb their darkest secrets. He paused for a moment and savored the familiar scents of the synagogue—human sweat, mingled with smoldering wicks and leather scrolls. When Jesus spoke, absolute certainty and authority permeated every word: "Today, this writing has been fulfilled in your hearing."

Shattered Assumptions

One of the pictures that Scripture paints about prayer is that it's hazardous, dangerous, utterly unsafe. Consider a few examples from Scripture:

Moses asked God for mercy—and spent the next four decades coddling a whining throng of ex-slaves across the desert.

Elijah prayed for fire—and found himself on Queen Jezebel's list of most-wanted criminals.

Isaiah cried, "Here am I, Lord; send me"—and, according to Jewish tradition, King Manasseh sawed him in half.

Jesus prayed, "May your will be done"—and spent six hours on a cross.

One summer evening, several Jews in Nazareth found out that the Amidah, one of the most important prayers in their synagogue liturgy, was especially hazardous.

The prayer seemed safe. The people had repeated the blessing every Sabbath since their childhood. Yet one snippet from this prayer was more dangerous than a bucket of water balloons in the church bus. It was this simple phrase: "Dwell in Zion!"

Sounds harmless, doesn't it? That's what the Jews in Nazareth thought—until God answered their prayer. God's answer to this obscure plea in the middle of the *Amidah* shattered the people's assumptions about how God works.

The "Limits" of Zion

In the Amidah, "Zion" referred not only to the craggy hill where Solomon had constructed a temple; it also pointed to the people of God. This connotation was as ancient as the book of Isaiah:

Zion says, "The Lord has forsaken me, my Lord has forgotten me...." "I could never forget you. See, I have engraved you on the palms of my hands.... I will raise my hand to the nations and lift up my ensign to peoples. They will bring your sons in their bosoms, and carry your daughters on their backs."

ISAIAH 49:14, 16, 22

The author of Hebrews echoed Isaiah's understanding of Zion. He defined Zion as "the assembly of the firstborn, enrolled in heaven" (Heb 12:22–23).

This much, the Nazarenes understood: When they said, "Dwell in Zion," they were asking God to live in peace, to pitch his tent, among his people.

The Nazarenes could even handle the idea that Jesus was God's chosen representative. When Jesus said, "Today, this writing has been fulfilled in your hearing," they didn't balk. Instead, "all the people testified about him and expressed amazement at the gracious words that flowed from his mouth" (Lk 4:21–22). Sure, they expressed some doubt, yet they remained willing to listen and to wait for a miracle. Then came the clincher: God's works of wonder were not for the Jews alone—they were for anyone who would submit to God's ways.

> And [Jesus] said, "In truth, I say to you, many widows lived in Israel in the days of Elijah, when the sky was closed for three years and six months, when a great drought came over the whole land. Yet Elijah was sent to none of them. He was sent only to Zarephath, in the land of Sidon, to a woman who was a widow. Many lepers lived in Israel in the time of Elisha the prophet. Yet none of them was cleansed except Naaman the Syrian." Then, everyone in the synagogue was filled with wrath.
>
> LUKE 4:24-28

The Nazarenes had prayed, "Dwell in Zion!" and God had answered their prayer. In the words of the apostle John, "The Word became flesh and dwelt among them" (Jn 1:14). But God pitched his tent on his own terms and in his own way. The Nazarenes simply couldn't stomach the thought that God might drive his tent-stakes beyond the Jewish people. And the one thing that Naaman and the widow from Sidon held in common was that they were both Gentiles. The hometown boy's words shattered the homogeneous-unit principle that drove the Nazarenes' congregational growth strategy. In their minds, Zion might encompass the poor, the blind, the imprisoned, and the oppressed—but never could Zion embrace a Gentile. Yet according to Jesus, God's target audience included *all* sorts of people:

Sidonian widows and Syrian army officers.

Roman centurions and sticky-fingered tax collectors.

Pious hypocrites and filthy prostitutes.

People who cart seventeen items through the ten-items-or-less express lane.

The neighbor whose dog gets on your nerves.

The driver who cuts me off on the 193rd Street exit ramp.

All sorts of people.

Living the Amidah

"Dwell in Zion!" If contemporary Christians learned to live this plea from the Amidah, what would change? Perhaps we would recognize that the hardest aspect of prayer is neither learning to pray nor receiving an answer to our prayers. The most difficult part of prayer is recognizing and accepting the answers when they come. The Nazarenes prayed, "Dwell in Zion!" and God did, but he didn't dwell among them in quite the way they expected he would. Whenever God reveals his presence among his people—whenever God "dwells in Zion"—his people's assumptions about his ways usually end up shattered.

When this happens we are forced to choose between two paths: Will we recognize and accept the unwelcome answers to our prayers, even though these answers may cost us deeply? Or will we, like the Jews in Nazareth, clench so tightly to our misguided assumptions that we can't see the answer to our prayers even when the answer is standing in front of us?

I know which path I usually take. I suspect it's the same well-worn path that you've taken more often than you care to admit. In Nazareth, the path led to the edge of a cliff: "Everyone in the synagogue was filled with wrath.... They took Jesus to the edge of the hill on which their city was built, intending to throw him off the cliff" (Lk 4:28-29). In our lives, the path usually leads either to prayers that are unsafe but insincere or prayers that are safe but petty. In the first case, our prayers are lies; in the second case, our prayers are empty. In both cases, we fail to experience God's presence among his people.

Prayer as Meaningless Ritual

I recall one week when I realized how frequently my prayers were "unsafe but insincere" rituals. I was struggling to balance my seminary studies with my responsibilities as the pastor of a small church. Our aging Ford Escort had stripped a timing belt. I had failed to finish an important assignment because of our car problems. When my wife and I arrived home Friday evening, an insufficient-funds notice greeted us from our mailbox.

When we sat at the table to eat dinner that evening, I was disheartened, discouraged, and depressed. Yet a curious combination of custom and commitment compelled me to say a blessing. I drew a deep breath and recited the familiar cliché, "Lord, I thank you for this day and for...."

I stopped. *What am I thinking? Thank God for this day? I'm not thankful for today. In fact, I wish I could have skipped this entire week. How can I be thankful for stalled cars, stingy churches, and short checking balances? I don't even want to be thankful!* I had prayed pious words, but I hadn't meant a single word I'd said.

The dilemma doesn't only occur at dinner tables at the end of no-good, awful, rotten days. It also happens when we don't like God's answers to our prayers. Consider the words of the Amidah: "You are blessed, *Adonai!*... Dwell in Zion!... We serve you in reverent fear." Remember the meaning of "blessed"? The same Hebrew word means "to bless" and "to bow." We cannot sincerely bless God's name without bowing to God's will. The Nazarenes who heard Jesus in the synagogue that day were more than willing to bless the Lord—until bowing to God's identity required them to submit to a hometown boy's claim that God's covenant could include Gentiles. Yet the reason that God had defied their expectations was because he longed to give them something *greater* than their expectations.

He does the same for us. When I resist God's unexpected answers to my prayers, I am like a child born in 1895 whose father promised him a horse for his twenty-first birthday. Suppose that, in 1916, the son received a Model-T Ford instead. "It would be a strange son who would accuse his father of breaking his promise just because there was no horse," writes Christopher J.H. Wright. "It is obvious that ... the father has more than kept his promise. In fact he has done so in a way that *surpasses* the original words of the promise."[7]

That's how God answers our prayers. Whenever his answer *defies* our expectations, it also *surpasses* our expectations. Yet how do we respond? Look again at Luke 4: "Then, everyone in the synagogue was filled with wrath. They leaped to their feet and forced Jesus out of town. They took him to the edge of the hill on which their city was built, intending to throw him off the cliff."

When our prayers are insincere, we would rather grovel in the muck of our own barren fantasies than embrace the reality of a God who gives us his best only when we are willing to leave the choice to him. We would rather shove God off the edge of a cliff than lay our greed and self-indulgence at his nail-scarred feet. "Surrender don't come natural to me," a contemporary psalmist wrote. "I'd rather fight You for something I don't really want than to take what You give that I need."[8] Deep inside, in the moments when I am painfully honest, so would I.

Prayer as Personal Pacifier

In our attempt to avoid insincere prayers, Christians frequently go to the other extreme—praying prayers that are sincere but petty. Consider the requests shared at a typical prayer meeting:

"Keep my grandma safe as she travels."

"I really need God's help to pass this exam."

"My brother-in-law's cousin's aunt has an ingrown toenail."

I'm not saying that these requests are wrong: God does care about smarting toenails, safe travels, and science tests. But when our times of prayer focus primarily on personal needs, we are settling for less than what God intended. Like an infant's pacifier, prayer becomes a gadget that brings fleeting gratification but never helps us grow. The result is that we settle for too little in our Christian lives. C.S. Lewis described our dilemma in this way:

> If we consider the unblushing promises of reward and the staggering nature of the rewards promised in the Gospels, it would seem that Our Lord finds our desires not too strong, but too weak. Like an ignorant child who wants to go on making mud pies in a slum because he cannot imagine what

is meant by the offer of a holiday at the sea, we are half-hearted creatures, fooling about with drink and sex and ambition when infinite joy is offered us. We are far too easily pleased.[9]

We are like the tourist who traveled to Switzerland, longing to meet the foremost theologian of the twentieth century, Karl Barth. The tourist boarded a bus and unwittingly sat beside Barth. "What do you want to see in our city?" Barth asked the man.

He replied, "I would like to see the great theologian, Karl Barth. Do you know him?"

"Oh yes," said Barth, "I shave him every morning."

The tourist left the bus ecstatic, telling his friends that he had met Barth's barber, when he could have enjoyed an encounter with Barth himself.[10] In the same way, when we stop at prayers for toenails and tests and safe travels, never moving beyond our petty pangs, we never experience the glorious presence of God.

Why do we remain satisfied with sincere yet petty prayers? Suppose that we did sincerely and passionately pray, "Lord, do whatever it takes to reveal yourself among us." What might happen then? God revealed his glory on Mount Sinai, and an entire nation screamed, "Don't let God speak to us, or we will die!" God revealed the full extent of his love in Jesus Christ, and all humanity shrieked, "Crucify him!" God revealed his Spirit at Pentecost and in a matter of months, the preachers found themselves in prison, a deacon ended up dead, and two principal donors to the church's benevolence fund left Peter's office on stretchers (see Acts 5:1–11, 18; 8:2). Is it any wonder that we settle for secondhand encounters with God?

There is a reason why authentic prayer is unsafe: it brings us into the presence of a God who is unsafe, into the presence of a God who can never be domesticated or reduced to fit into the petty plans of his people.

Remember this scene from *The Lion, the Witch, and the Wardrobe?*

> "If there's anyone who can appear before Aslan without their knees knocking, they're either braver than most or just silly," said Mrs. Beaver.
> "Then he isn't safe?" said Lucy.
> "Safe?" said Mr. Beaver. "Don't you hear what Mrs. Beaver tells you? Who said anything about safe? 'Course he isn't safe. But he's good. He's the King, I tell you."[11]

Answers to authentic prayers, like the God who grants them, are never safe but always good.

The Greatest Gift of All

To ask God to dwell in Zion is to ask him to reveal his presence among his people. His presence may bring a few unwelcome answers. Who knows? It may even shatter a few of our assumptions—assumptions about whom God can forgive and how God can work. And yet we have God's assurance that his gifts—even the unwelcome ones—are always good:

> Is there anyone among you who, if your child asks for a fish, will give him a snake instead? Or if your child asks for an egg, will you give a scorpion? So if you who are evil have enough sense to give good gifts to your children, how much more will the heavenly Father give the Holy Spirit to those who ask him!
>
> LUKE 11:11–13

Yes, God always gives his children fish instead of snakes and eggs instead of scorpions, but the fish aren't always prepared as we expected and sometimes the eggs are hard-boiled. So, amid the answers that confound our expectations, God offers a greater gift ... the greatest gift of all ... the gift of himself. In the words of Frederick Buechner, "The God you call upon with even your most half-cocked and halting prayer will finally come down the path you beat, and even if he does not bring the answer you want, he will bring you himself."[12] Confronted by the living God, I must ask myself again: Will I embrace him as my Lord, whatever the cost? Or will I tread the well-worn trail that leads to the edge of the cliff? If I have sincerely asked him to dwell in Zion, there's only one choice.

——A MEDITATION——

Oh Lord, my God,
  the Highest God,
      the Creator of heaven and earth,
        my Shield and the Shield of my ancestors—
It's easy to ask you to dwell in Zion.
  It's tough to ask you to dwell in me.
I *want* you to dwell in my life—
  I think.
But there are so many dirty corners,
  so many dark crannies,
      so many prejudices and preconceptions
        that only you can see.
Do I really want you to dwell in my life—
  even if it hurts?
Do I really want you to transform me—
  whatever the cost?
Do I really want *you?*
  I hope so.
Yet I need so much more than hope.
  I need help.
      I need *you.*
Amen.

Pray then in this way: "Our Father in heaven, hallowed be your name. Your kingdom come. Your will be done, on earth as it is in heaven. Give us this day our daily bread. And forgive us our debts, as we also have forgiven our debtors. And do not bring us to the time of trial, but rescue us from the evil one."

The Lord's Prayer,
MATTHEW 6:9–13, NRSV

May his great name be magnified and hallowed in the world which he created according to his will. May he make his kingship sovereign in your lifetime and in your days, speedily and soon.[1]

Opening lines of the *Kaddish*,
spoken at memorial services
and at the close of the synagogue service

Our God and the God of our fathers,... remove our guilt and blot out our iniquities, as you have promised.... You are blessed, *Adonai*—he who forgives transgressions, the king of the universe, the one who sanctifies Israel and the Day of Atonement.[2]

Traditional Jewish Prayer
spoken on Yom Kippur, the Day of Atonement

Lead me not into sin, or into iniquity, or into temptation. And may the good inclination have sway over me and let not the evil inclination have sway over me.[3]

Traditional Jewish Prayer

CHAPTER FIVE

Looking for the Kingdom:
The Lord's Prayer and the Prayers in the Garden

The big fisherman stopped for a moment when he reached the crest of the hill. He brushed an unruly black curl away from his eyes and glanced down the hillside. Heavy spring rains had washed over Galilee again, leaving long, sandy gouges in the slopes. The village of Capernaum meandered crookedly along the bottom of the hill. Smoke wandered upward from courtyards and rooftops and mingled with the morning fog to form a luminous haze in the sunlight.

Beyond the clusters of black basalt houses, the Sea of Galilee stretched southward, toward Samaria. The rising sun was already chasing away the silken wisps of fog that remained on the lake.[4] A half-dozen boats darted through the fading mist, toward the docks that dotted the rocky shore. Burly fishermen, bare-chested and sun-bronzed, stood in the bows, bellowing good-natured curses and grudging compliments at their competitors. Another night of fishing had ended. Now, the race was on. Merchants were already flocking to the docks, prepared to trade fistfuls of gleaming denarii for the slender barbels and stubby perches that writhed beneath the decks of the boats.

It was all so familiar to Simon. The pungent scents of fresh fish and lake water, the thrill of hauling a net, gorged with fish, into the boat.... So many years of mending nets and patching leaks, so many stormy nights on the sea, so many frantic dashes to the shore.... And now—what? He glimpsed his barren boat and his nets, decaying along the shore. Not for the first time, a deluge of doubt chilled his stomach.

At first, it had been an adventure—rambling across Galilee alongside the carpenter-turned-rabbi. Jesus' ideas were radical, revolutionary, maybe even messianic. Then, a few local simpletons claimed that the rabbi from Nazareth had healed them.[5] Suddenly the little flock of learners had erupted into a horde of crackpots and cripples, hustlers and whores.

Now, when Jesus spent the night in Simon's home in Capernaum,[6] the only person who rejoiced was the local tavern-keeper. After glutting themselves with wine, the swarm of ragamuffins slept in the streets around Simon's house—and did who-knows-what in the shadowed byways and alleys. Simon had become the laughingstock of Capernaum. His friends accused him of catching "messiah fever." His father had publicly labeled him a fool. The moneybag that dangled from his belt was limp. What else could following this rabbi possibly cost him?

"Simon! Simon Bar-Jonah!"

It was Andrew. Simon turned and pinpointed his younger brother at the center of the crowd, near the teacher's side. A few wealthy merchants had set up tents along the edges of the mob. The rest of the rabble sprawled in the sun, laughing and frolicking. The big fisherman ambled past the tents and arrived at Andrew's side just in time to see the teacher let a scrawny waif wrestle him to the ground. Jesus emerged from the cluster of toddlers and leaped to his feet, laughing. Then he lifted his hands. The crowd turned silent.

Simon sat on the ground between two of his former fishing partners. The teacher wandered among the people, embracing them one by one, whispering blessings to the children. Finally he returned to the center of the crowd. He squatted beside Simon and stared into his eyes. Simon squirmed and longed for a place to hide. Yet he sensed that no rock in all of Galilee could possibly shield him from Jesus' gaze. Somehow, Jesus seemed to sense every uncertainty, every misgiving, in Simon's heart. He ran his hand through Simon's beard and gripped the fisherman's bulky shoulder.

"Simon, are you poor?"

Jesus spoke gently, but every person in the crowd heard him clearly. Simon nodded sheepishly and tossed Jesus his empty money-bag. Jesus grinned at Simon and hurled the goatskin bag into the air. "Congratulations to you who are poor! God's kingdom belongs to you!"⁷

Laughter erupted throughout the crowd. Then a few folk glimpsed the seriousness in the teacher's eyes. The laughter faded into dumb-struck silence. Jesus wasn't joking.

He ruffled a grubby urchin's hair and asked, "Are you hungry?"

The boy nodded vigorously. Jesus seized the urchin in his arms and whirled toward the crowd:

"Congratulations to you who are famished now—you will be filled! Congratulations to you who are weeping now—you will laugh! Congratulations to you when others disdain you—when they reject you, revile you, and ridicule you because you follow this son of humanity who speaks to you now! Rejoice in that day and jump for joy! Surely your reward in heaven is great, because that's how their ancestors treated God's prophets."

Jesus released the boy and pointed to the tents at the edge of the crowd.

"As for those of you who are rich now—wretched are you! You have already received your comfort! Wretched are you who gorge yourselves with food now! You will go hungry. Wretched are those of you who laugh at others now! You will grieve and weep. Wretched are you when all people compliment you! That's how their ancestors treated the false prophets.

"To those of you who are still listening, I say this: Love your enemies, do good to those who despise you, bless those who curse you!"

Jesus scrambled up the side of a massive rock and sat on top of the stone. Silhouetted against the sapphire sky, his tan tunic snapping in the wind, he began to teach. His words rang across the hills like trumpet-blasts:

"When someone gives you a hard time, respond with the energies of prayer, for then you are working out of your true selves, your God-created selves.

"When you come before God, don't turn that into a theatrical production. All these people making a regular show out of their prayers, hoping for stardom! Do you think God sits in a box seat? Here's what I want you to do: Find a quiet, secluded place so you won't be tempted to role-play before God. Just be there as simply and honestly as you can manage. The focus will shift from you to God, and you will begin to sense his grace. With a God like this loving you, you can pray very simply. Like this ..."8

Jesus turned his face upward and stretched out his hands, smiling as he spoke: "'Our *Abba* in the heavens, may your name be recognized as holy. May your kingdom come. May your will be done on the earth just as it is in the heavens. Give us day-by-day our daily bread. Forgive us our debts, just as we forgive those who are indebted to us. Do not lead us into temptation. Deliver us from the evil one.'"

Simon exhaled slowly. How long had he been holding his breath? He didn't know. He glanced at the speechless throng around him. Their eyes were wide, their brows furrowed, their faces clenched like fists. "Abba" ... the carpenter had called God "our Abba." Not *"Adonai* our God, the king of the universe." Not even Ha'ab, "the Father." No, the carpenter had called God "our Abba."

The Signpost That Points Us Home

I still remember the first time I heard the Lord's Prayer recited in worship. It was so different from anything I had ever experienced before, utterly unfamiliar to a boy whose faith was forged in rural Missouri by the crude fervor of Baptist fundamentalism. Everyone else knew when to sit, when to stand, what to say when. I didn't. I had never heard a litany, never worshiped in a place where the pastor wore a robe, never recited the Lord's Prayer.

The minister's prayer over the bread and the cup seemed interminably long.

"So, we are bold to say ... "

At this point, all that I was bold to say was, "Is it almost over?"

"Our Father... "

Wait ... was that something familiar?

"... which art in heaven ... "

Even *I* had heard this part before.

"... hallowed be thy name."

I fumbled with the worship folder, trying to find the words. At first, I read them hesitantly. Then, I too became bold to speak this prayer.

"Thy kingdom come. Thy will be done... "

My voice merged with the multitude around me.

"...on earth as it is in heaven."

For a moment, human labels lost their meaning. No Presbyterians or Baptists, no Episcopalians or Catholics, were present in that place. We were simply a band of pilgrims who shared a common prayer because we had undertaken a common journey toward the kingdom of God.

In that moment, nearly a decade ago, I recognized that the Lord's Prayer is not simply a prayer. It is a *signpost*—a signpost that binds the people of God together and keeps them pointed toward God's kingdom.

The signposts of this world run us ragged, sending us puffing and panting after paltry kingdoms of pleasure and power. But amid the gaudy lights and the unbeatable deals that gild the world's billboards, one simple signpost, the Lord's Prayer, points us home. This prayer is the guide for our journey toward the kingdom of God. To understand this prayer in its context, we must first answer two questions: What did Jesus mean when he said, "Thy kingdom come"? And what made the Lord's Prayer different from other prayers of the first century?

Where Is "Thy Kingdom Come"?

Ever since the fiasco in the Garden of Eden, people have been longing for God's kingdom. Their journey always began in the same way: an unexplainable restlessness, a longing for an unknown place to which a divine voice seemed to be calling them, a yearning for a place where the reign of God was undisputed. Before the afflicted folk could ask where or why, they were headed for the Promised Land.

Or a burning bush.

Or Jerusalem.

Or the hills of Galilee.

Or the leper colonies of Calcutta.

Or the kneeling bench at the front of the sanctuary.

The destinations may differ, but the dream remains the same. It's the longing expressed in the Lord's Prayer: "May your kingdom come ... on earth." In other words, "May we find a place on earth where your presence is as evident as it is in the heavens."

Abraham was one of the first victims of this longing. Abraham's father, Terah, had sensed the restlessness first. One day, he piled his belongings and his children on the humps of his favorite camels and headed out from Ur to Haran—the ancient equivalent of a trip from Philadelphia to Phoenix. When they reached Haran, Terah's energy and the camels' patience were all but gone. So Terah settled down in Haran long enough to die there. Maybe Abraham and Sarah tried to settle down too. Maybe they laid a foundation beneath their tent, planted some shrubbery around the entrance, and joined a civic club. It didn't last. Before long, Sarah found Abraham out behind the tent, sitting on his camel, staring into the sunset. She recognized that restless look in his eyes. The look that said no matter where they were, they weren't *there* yet. The look that said he could see "thy kingdom come," but only in the distance, just past the horizon.[9]

Finally, God told Abraham that it was time to load up the camels again: "Leave your country, your family, and your father's household, and go to the land that I will show you" (Gn 12:2). According to the author of Hebrews, "Abraham was looking for the city that has a real foundation, whose architect and builder is God.... All these people wanted the same thing—a better domain, a heavenly domain" (Heb 11:10, 16). They were searching for "thy kingdom come."

The problem was, neither Abraham nor his descendants were certain what God's kingdom was or where they could find it. So they wandered from Haran to Canaan, from Canaan to Egypt, across the Sinai peninsula, to the rivers of Babylon and back again. It's no wonder that the first words the Hebrews spoke when they entered the Promised Land were, "My father was a wandering Aramean" (see Dt 26:1–11). Restlessness was in their blood.

By the time John the Baptist started preaching along Jordan's banks, the Israelites weren't traveling anymore. Yet they were still waiting, yearning, aching, for "the city that is to come" (Heb 13:14). Every first-century Jew, including Jesus and his disciples, prayed the same prayer at the end of every synagogue service: "Blessed be ... the king of the universe.... May he make his kingship sovereign in your lifetime." In other words, "thy kingdom come."

What Abraham and the children of Israel and the first disciples of Jesus couldn't comprehend was that they were not hungering for a kingdom they could touch or taste or feel. Jesus finally made the matter clear: "The kingdom of God isn't coming with things that you can see. No one can say, 'Look! Here it is!' or 'There it is!' For, in fact, the kingdom of God is among you."[10]

"The kingdom of God is among you." The kingdom that you have craved so long is *among you.* Among you in the flesh of the carpenter from Nazareth (see Jn 10:38; 14:6-11,20). The kingdom is *among you,* for the kingdom is the presence of the Father.[11] Nothing more, nothing less.

Ancient kings might declare, in moments of drunken passion, "Ask me anything you wish, up to half of my kingdom, and I will give it to you!" Through the Lord's Prayer, the king of the universe declares to his children, "Ask me anything you wish. You can never ask for more than I have already given to you. For my presence *is* my kingdom, and through Jesus Christ, that is precisely what I have given to you."

What Makes the Lord's Prayer Different?

When I pray the words "thy kingdom come," I am not praying for my personal vision of paradise. By praying this prayer, I implicitly admit that only the One who was fully present in Jesus Christ can possibly fulfill my deepest longings. I am praying for the presence of my heavenly Father. This focus on the Father is what made the Lord's Prayer different from any prayer that the disciples had ever heard before.

Most of the lines from the Lord's Prayer were vaguely familiar to the disciples. At least once every week, faithful Jews recited the *Kaddish*—"May his great name be magnified and hallowed.... May he make his kingship sovereign in your lifetime."[12] On Yom Kippur they prayed, "Pardon our transgressions." In times of temptation they whispered, "Lead me not into sin, or into iniquity, or into temptation." "Hallowed be thy name." "Thy kingdom come." "Forgive us our debts." "Lead us not into temptation." All of them were familiar concepts to Jesus and his disciples.

So what made the Lord's Prayer different?

One simple phrase ...

"Our Father."

Only in the Lord's Prayer did Jesus call his Father "*our* Father."[13] His original words were probably even more overwhelming. More than likely, Jesus called his Father *Abba*—an Aramaic appellation that combined tender intimacy with profound respect. Every child in Judea addressed her father as Abba, but no one ever addressed God in this way.

By commanding his disciples to pray "our Abba," Jesus was inviting them to enjoy the same intimate relationship with the Father that Jesus had experienced in eternity past. No parallel to these words exists in any other world religion.[14] No Muslim would dream of addressing Allah as "our Abba"—Allah is powerful but not tender. No Hindu would consider calling the Brahmin "our Abba"—the divine life-force is universal but not personal. The Jews referred to God as "our Father" but never as "our Abba."[15] "Our Abba" places the Lord's Prayer in a category by itself.

To pray "our Abba" is to pray as a child. "Unless you become like children," Jesus once commented to his disciples, "you'll never make it into the kingdom" (Mt 18:2). Another time, he laughed, looked toward the sky, and said, "Thank you, Abba, Lord of heaven and earth! You hid your plans from the wise and intelligent and revealed them to babies. Yes, Abba! This was your gracious will" (Lk 10:21).

What does it mean to pray as a child? In the first-century world, to be a child was not to be naive or to possess "childlike faith." To be a child was *to have no rights.*

> In the present day, we tend to idealize childhood as the happy age of innocence, insouciance, and simple faith.... The New Testament world was not sentimental about children and had no illusion about any pretended innate goodness in them.... In New Testament times, the child was considered of no importance, meriting little attention or favor. Children in that society had no status at all—they did not count.[16]

Under the Roman law of *patria potestas,* the father held complete control over every part of his child's life. If a first-century father did not want his newborn child, he "exposed" the infant— he left the baby to die in a deserted field. Children could neither possess their own property nor choose their own mates. Even when a child was grown, the patriarch of the household could legally exile or execute his offspring. Whether a child lived or died, ate or starved, succeeded or failed—*everything* in a child's life depended on the will of his or her father.[17]

The nineteenth-century saint Thérèse of Lisieux described the life of childlike trust in our heavenly Father in this way: "It is recognizing one's nothingness, expecting everything from the good God, just as a little child expects everything from its father; it is not getting anxious about anything.... It is never being disheartened by one's faults, because children often fall, but they are too little to do themselves much harm."[18]

To pray as a child is to pray as if everything in my life depends on my heavenly Abba. Then, I no longer need to look for "thy kingdom come." The kingdom has come in me. For the presence of Abba *is* the kingdom, and the Father chooses to be present whenever and wherever his children recognize their dependence on him.

Living in Dependence on Abba

So, what does it mean to live in absolute dependence on our heavenly Abba? I think we find the answer not in any teachings about prayer but in an unexpected time and an unlikely place—in the tormented cries of Jesus in the Garden of Gethsemane (see Mk 14:35–36). In the words of Walter Wangerin,

> What takes place in the Garden of Gethsemane is the Lord's Prayer actually *happening,* as though the earlier words were a script and this is the drama itself....
>
> In the garden, Jesus, now more than ever in his ministry, is the living embodiment of the second petition, *Thy kingdom come.* Right now, his acceptance of the Father's will *is* the coming of the kingdom here.

And he begins both prayers the same. But whereas the first might have seemed a formal address to "Our Father," this latter cry is a howl, a spontaneous, needful plea: "*Abba*, Father!" Here is a child who cannot survive apart from this relationship. By crying "*Abba!*" he hurls himself at the holy parent: he runs like a child; like a child he begs attention; but also like a child he trusts his daddy to do right and well.

When Jesus teaches us to pray, he does not teach plain recitation. Rather, he calls us to a way of being. He makes of prayer a doing. And by his own extreme example, he shows that prayer is the active relationship between ourselves, dear little children, and the dear Father, *Abba*.[19]

If the prayers in the garden *are* the Lord's Prayer in action, it was the Lord's Prayer that led Jesus to the cross. At this point, the Lord's Prayer is a source of comfort, reminding me that God is still my Father, even in my darkest moments. Yet the prayer also terrifies me. If Jesus prayed, "*Abba*, thy will be done," and ended up on a cross, what might the Lord's Prayer cost me?

My dependence on myself? It cannot coexist with *Abba*, the word that declares my absolute dependence on the heavenly Father.

My obsessions with titles to list behind my signature and accomplishments to adorn my curriculum vitae? They must crumble under the weight of "hallowed be *thy* name."

My longing for larger numbers to scribble on line seven of my 1040 form? It cannot stand when I sincerely pray for "daily bread"—what I need for today and tomorrow, nothing more.

My conviction that I have the right to withhold forgiveness from the not-quite-divine folk in my church? "Forgive us our debts as we forgive our debtors" shatters that delusion.

My flirtations with the fringes of sin? They cannot remain when I pray, "Deliver us from evil."

That's what it means to embrace Abba's presence, to embark on the journey to "kingdom come."

A few weeks ago, I received an advertisement from a prominent evangelical publisher. The heading declared, "Risk-free devotional materials!" If I am honest with myself, that's what I want sometimes when I repeat the Lord's Prayer—a painless prayer that comforts me but never challenges me. A risk-free recitation to hang on my wall. Yet that is precisely what the Lord's Prayer refuses to deliver. Prayed sincerely, the Lord's Prayer is risky. Its demands are unnatural, unreasonable, and uncomfortable. It is not a prayer for the faint-hearted. Neither is it a prayer for persons who want all the pleasures of a trip to hell without the unpleasant side effects. When we pray "our Father in the heavens ... may your kingdom come," we embark on a brutal journey that will not end until eternity begins. The journey is brutal because Abba refuses to postpone his kingdom until the end of time. To pray the Lord's Prayer is to ask Abba to be fully present here and now, in us. When Abba is present in our lives, we become the realm in which God is hallowing his name. Then nothing, absolutely nothing, can remain the same.

> We do well not to pray the Lord's Prayer lightly. It takes guts to pray it at all.... "Thy will be done" is what we are saying.... We are asking God to be God. We are asking God to do not what we want but what God wants.... "Thy kingdom come ... on earth" is what we are saying. And if that were to suddenly happen, what then? What would stand and what would fall?... Which if any of our most precious visions of who God is and of what human beings are would prove to be

more or less on the mark and which would turn out to be phony as three-dollar bills?... It is only the words "Our Father" that make the prayer bearable. If God is indeed something like a father, then as something like children maybe we can risk approaching him anyway.[20]

——A Meditation——

Our *Abba* in the heavens,
When I call you "my God,"
   I can make-believe that you are my property.
When I call you "my King,"
   I can make-believe that I am your prince.
Only when I whisper "our *Abba*,"
   do I know who I am.
I am Abba's child.
   Nothing more.
      Nothing less.
         Simply, only, Abba's little boy.
Grimy face, grubby hands
   from building my own kingdoms—
      they always crumble, mud and sand,
         when your presence washes over them.
I didn't like them either,
   but your kingdom seemed so far away.
      Please, Abba, make your kingdom come in me.
      Please, Abba, become my hope, my home.
         Amen.

——THE PRAYER AT THE TOMB OF LAZARUS——

When Jesus arrived, he found that Lazarus had already been in the tomb four days.... It was a cave, and a stone was lying against it.... Jesus looked upward and said, "Father, I thank you for having heard me. I knew that you always hear me, but I have said this for the sake of the crowd standing here, so that they may believe that you sent me." When he had said this, he cried with a loud voice, "Lazarus, come out!"

JOHN 11:17, 38, 41-43, NRSV

CHAPTER SIX

The God Who Hears:
The Prayer at the Tomb of Lazarus

The band of learners meandered behind their teacher, up the southeastern slope of the Mount of Olives. After two days of traveling, they finally caught sight of Bethany. Still, no one spoke. The disciples stared silently toward the village, squinting their eyes in the late afternoon sun. The rabbi told no riddles, Simon spoke no confessions, James had no jokes, and John had no questions— none that he knew how to ask, anyway.

Suddenly, Simon heard the rhythmic sound of sandal soles slapping against the road that led to Bethany. When he looked up, he saw a woman in the distance, sprinting toward them like a frightened hare.

It was Mary.

Mary, the sister of Martha.

Mary, the one whose brother was dead.

Simon watched the puffs of dust rise and fade beneath her feet as she ran down the dusty road. When Jesus saw her face, his chin quivered beneath his beard. Her eyes were bloodshot and swollen, and her sackcloth tunic was torn. Sweat and tears had mingled with the ashes on her cheeks and turned her skin deathly gray. When she reached Jesus, she lunged forward and seized his feet.

"My Lord ..." It was the ragged gasp of a woman who had wept until no tears remained. "If only you had been here, my brother ... my brother wouldn't have died."

Jesus slid to his knees, and Mary fell, heaving, against his chest. The carpenter's hands gently smoothed the tangled hair that had slipped out of her veil.

Mary sobbed and moaned, but her eyes remained dry. "If only ... if only ... oh Lazarus!"

Within moments, the cries of a mourning crowd and the wailing of a pair of flutes surrounded the disciples.[1] The mourners pitched dust in the air, the flutists performed their dirges, and the carpenter from Nazareth buried his face in his hands. The lamentations echoed around Mary and Jesus: "May the Master of consolations comfort you!" "Blessed be the one who comforts the mourners!"[2]

"Where did you lay him?" the rabbi murmured.

"Lord." It was Martha who answered him. "Come and see."

Jesus stood and lifted Mary to her feet. When he looked into her eyes, grief surged from the depths of his body. His shoulders began to convulse, and his chin dropped to his chest. He clutched the two sisters, as if he would collapse without them. The threesome stumbled toward the garden arm-in-arm, a living chain of sorrows.

When they reached the garden, the rabbi turned to a nearby mourner. "Run ahead and roll away the stone." The man was gone before Martha could protest.

"Lord, it's too late for you to see him now. He has been dead ..." Martha choked on her words; when she recovered her voice, a hint of bitterness burst from the lump in her throat. "He has been dead for four days. The tomb already reeks!"

"I told you," the voice of Jesus was firm despite his tears, "if you believe, you will see God's glory."

The stone was already gone when they reached the garden. A dark, gaping hole stared at the crowd of mourners. When Mary and Martha saw the open tomb, they crumpled to the ground. Jesus remained standing.

He looked upward and declared, "Abba, thank you for having heard me. I knew that you always hear me, but I have said this for the sake of the crowd standing here, so they will believe that you sent me." When Jesus turned toward the tomb, even the birds were silent.

The look in the rabbi's eyes shifted from sorrow to defiance.

Without warning, he lifted his hands and cried, "Lazarus! Come out!"

Martha bristled at the Galilean carpenter's callousness. Mary simply cried ... until she heard an unfamiliar rustling and dared to stare once more into the mouth of the cave. She saw someone standing inside the tomb. What she saw didn't stop her tears—the tears, in fact, continued for several days—but it did change the reason for her weeping.

The Listening God

Rayann's intentions were good. To celebrate the birthday of a certain *Star Wars* fanatic whom she had recently married, she baked a cookie in the shape of an Imperial Star Destroyer. I had asked for a *Star Wars* cake, so when I saw the resulting conglomeration of sugary dough, gray-blue icing, and chocolate chips, I laughed and thanked her several times. It was a thoughtful gift; I appreciated it—and it *did* look like a starship!

Unfortunately, the similarities between the cookie and a Star Destroyer didn't stop with the outward appearance. The taste and texture of the cookie were more like the titanium hull of a starship than I care to recall. And the smell ... well, I've never actually sniffed the exhaust from a hyper-drive, but I'm sure this scent was fairly close. Somewhere between the mixing bowl and the table, something had gone desperately wrong with this culinary endeavor. After two days of chewing, the dog deduced that it was a Mesozoic fossil and returned it to the bowels of the earth where it belonged.[3]

Despite the damage to my digestive system, I was thankful for Rayann's gift. She had listened to my request. As I reflected on the incident, it occurred to me that perhaps God the Father yearns for me to respond to him in the same way. He doesn't want me to thank him because he always gives me what I want—after all, he *doesn't* always give me what I want. He wants me to thank him because he has taken the time to listen to me. He wants to hear my prayers of gratitude not because of *what he gives* but because of *who he is.*

That's why the prayer that Jesus prayed at Lazarus' tomb is so significant. Jesus didn't speak this prayer of gratitude after Lazarus lurched into the garden, full of life. When Jesus prayed this prayer, the body of Lazarus was still decomposing in the darkness of a cave. After four days among the dead, Lazarus was a reeking mass of half-decayed flesh.

So if Lazarus was still dead, why did Jesus thank his Abba?

Was it because Jesus was certain that God the Father would raise Lazarus from the dead? I don't think so. Believe it or not, God the Son didn't always receive positive responses to his prayers. Remember the prayer Jesus prayed for his future followers? "I pray ... that all of them may be one.... May they be brought to perfect unity" (Jn 17:20–23). Count the listings located under the word *church* in your local Yellow Pages, and you'll quickly discover how far God's people are from a positive answer to this prayer. Remember Jesus' prayer in the Garden of Gethsemane? "Abba," he cried, "remove this cup from me" (Mk 14:36). God the Father heard this prayer, God the Father answered this prayer—and God's answer was *no*.

When Jesus asked his Abba to raise Lazarus from the dead, he had no guarantee that the answer would be *yes*. All he had was an assurance that his Abba would do whatever was necessary to glorify his name (see Jn 11:4, 40; 12:27–28).

If an impending resurrection wasn't the prime motive for Jesus' prayer of gratitude, why did he thank his Abba? Jesus thanked God simply for hearing him: "Abba," he prayed, "thank you for having heard me.... You always hear me."

What had God the Father heard? Perhaps it was Jesus' promise to Martha that she would see God's glory (see Jn 11:40). Or perhaps it was an unspoken prayer for the resurrection of Lazarus. I think there's an answer that's more probable than either of these options, though: Jesus thanked his Abba for hearing his tears.

Chaos had erupted around the tomb of Lazarus. The mourners wailed their words of comfort while the flutists played their mourning songs. The sisters felt abandoned and the disciples felt afraid. And God the Son? According to John, "Jesus wept" (Jn 11:35). He couldn't put his prayers into words, so he put them into tears instead. And God the Father heard his cries.

Ever been there? Ever found yourself standing at the foot of a casket or trembling in the waiting room of a hospital, unable to pray but fully able to cry?

Even when our minds can't find the words to express our desires, our tears express our despair. The message of Jesus' prayer of gratitude is that God hears these prayers too. In the words of the apostle

Paul, "the Spirit helps us in our weakness. We don't always know how to pray the way we should. So, the very Spirit of God intercedes for us with groans that go beyond human language" (Rom 8:26).

I think that's why Jesus prayed, "Abba, thank you for having heard me." It wasn't because of any answer that his Abba had given him—he hadn't received any answers yet. It wasn't because he knew that he would kiss his friend again before the day ended. No, he prayed this prayer because, amid the chaos and confusion of a crowd that couldn't see beyond the coldness of Lazarus' corpse, God the Father heard the sobs of his Son. Not only did God the Father hear this garbled prayer, but he also answered—and his reply flooded Lazarus' tomb with more life than any cave on earth could possibly contain. From a cosmic perspective, a few tears shed over a single corpse seem fairly insignificant. And yet, in the plan of God, these tears became a prayer that was worthy of being answered.

God and Our "Stupid Problems"

Basketball bad boy Dennis Rodman once commented, "If there is a supreme being, he/she/it has a hell of a lot more to worry about than my stupid problems."[4] In one sense, Rodman was right: God has more important issues to deal with than my pathetic problems.

Why should the one whose fingertips swirl solar systems around their suns listen to me blubber about my shattered dreams?

Why should the one who dances with the supernovas stop to hear me cry?

Why should the one who endured the pain of the cross care about the paltry paroxysms of my soul?

Why should God pay attention to me?

The honest answer to these questions is that he shouldn't. Yet the message of Jesus' prayer of gratitude is that he does. For reasons that I still haven't figured out, my "stupid problems" are precisely what God *is* concerned about. In fact, the pangs and problems of this world concern God so deeply that when he stood face-to-face with them, he cried.

> This is a world where robins die, and sparrows, and people: the ones we love, the ones Jesus loves. All of them. They fall to the ground, they are enfolded into the earth. And most times, Jesus doesn't come to raise them up, not in our life-time, not so that we see....
>
> And where is Jesus—this one "who was to come into the world"? What does Jesus think? What does Jesus feel about a world like this? "Jesus wept."[5]

Yes, Jesus wept—but he did more than weep. He thanked his Abba for hearing his sobs and for turning them into a prayer. And in the moments when tears flow more readily than words, you, too, can offer thanks.

Living the Prayer

If you want to locate me at my church, look for a gaggle of middle-school girls. Wherever I go, a cluster of sixth- and seventh-grade girls usually trails behind me. I used to think that they followed me because I have a tendency to spend money on them whenever they ask. (My wife says that when a little girl asks for something, I'm a pushover. Just between you and me, she's probably right.) Then I noticed that even when I didn't have the money to buy them ice cream or the time to take them to play laser-tag, they still stuck with me.

One Sunday, Amanda met me in the hall, and I asked her, "Where are you headed?"

She hugged me and said, "Wherever you're going."

"Why do you guys always follow me everywhere?" I smiled at her.

She thought for a moment, tossed her hair over her shoulder, and said, "Because you always listen to us. You treat us like real people, even though we're just kids."

Is that, perhaps, how I should look at God? He doesn't always take me where I want to go, and he doesn't always spend his riches according to my requests. Sometimes his answers to my prayers bring joy, and sometimes his answers are as tough and bitter as a charred chocolate-chip cookie. But he *does* always listen to me. And so I keep tagging along behind him—even when his answer to my requests is *no*. Why? Perhaps it's because at the secret heart of all our prayers, what we really want is not an answer but an assurance—an assurance that our Abba is listening. The prayer of Jesus in the garden is our assurance that he is.

——A Meditation——

My Abba ...

Can your hear me?

Are you listening?

Or do you have more pressing matters to attend to?

A choir rehearsal with Gabriel, perhaps?

A strategy session meeting with Michael?

A review of the newly born solar systems?

Aren't they more significant than my pathetic pleas?

Yet ... you *are* listening, aren't you?

You really *hear* me, don't you?

You're paying attention to *me!*

I thought you would have better taste.

I thought you would have the sense to ignore

people like me.

But you don't,

and I am *so* glad.

Thank you, Abba, for listening to

people who don't deserve to be heard.

Thank you, Abba, for listening to

people like me.

Thank you, Abba.

Amen.

III.

KNOWING THE GOD WHO CREATES COMMUNITY

The Christian life is tough—
God knows, it's too tough to do alone.
That's why Jesus didn't call isolated individuals to follow him.
He called a group of disciples.
    He gathered a crowd.[1]

God is still gathering that crowd,
    still pulling us together,
        still trying to make us one
            through the Holy Sacraments,
            through his Holy Spirit,
                and through the prayers of his Holy Son.

"Why is this night different from all other nights? On all other nights we eat leavened or unleavened bread; on this night we eat only unleavened bread. On all other nights we eat all sorts of herbs; on this night we eat only bitter herbs. On all other nights we eat meat roasted, stewed, or boiled; on this night we eat only roasted meat. Why is this night different from all other nights?"

"My father was a wandering Aramean. He went down into Egypt with meager numbers and sojourned there. There he became a great and very populous nation. The Egyptians dealt harshly with us and oppressed us. They imposed heavy labor on us. We cried to *Adonai* the God of our ancestors, and *Adonai* heard our plea and saw our plight, our pain, and our oppression. *Adonai* freed us from Egypt by a mighty hand, by an outstretched arm, and awesome power, and with signs and wonders.

"This is the sacrifice of the Passover of *Adonai*, for he passed over the houses of the people of Israel in Egypt when he slaughtered the Egyptians but spared our houses. We were Pharaoh's slaves in Egypt, and *Adonai* our God brought us forth from there with a mighty hand and an outstretched arm. And if the Holy One, may he be blessed, had not brought our ancestors out of Egypt, then we, our children and our grandchildren, would still be Pharaoh's slaves in Egypt."

Question and response from a Passover liturgy[2]

"You are blessed, *Adonai* our God, king of the universe—he who, in his goodness, feeds the whole world with grace, kindness, and mercy. He gives food to all flesh, for his kindness is everlasting. You are blessed, *Adonai*—he who provides food for all.

"We thank you, *Adonai* our God, for having given our ancestors a heritage—a precious, good, and spacious land; for having brought us out from the land of Egypt and redeemed us from the house of slavery; for your covenant which you have sealed in our flesh; for your Torah which you have taught us; for your statutes which you have revealed to us; for the life, favor, and kindness which you have graciously given to us; and for the food we eat with which you constantly feed and sustain us every day, at all times, and at every hour.

"Our God and the God of our ancestors, may there rise and come and approach and be seen, accepted, heard, recollected, and remembered, the remembrance of us and the recollection of us, and the remembrance of our ancestors, and the remembrance of the Messiah, the descendant of David your servant, and the remembrance of Jerusalem, your holy city, and the remembrance of all your people, the house of Israel. May their remembrance come before you for life and for peace on this Festival of Unleavened Bread."

Birkat Ha-Mazon[3]
Blessing spoken after the Passover meal

CHAPTER SEVEN

The God Who Remembers:
The Prayer of Passover

Were they ready?

I glanced around the wooden doorframe. Oil lamps tossed shadows carelessly across the walls of the Upper Room. The rabbi and his followers had finished their first cup of wine. Now they reclined around the table on linen cushions stuffed with wool.

"I tell you," Jesus was saying, "whoever receives anyone whom I send receives me. And whoever receives me receives the one who sent me."[4]

Was it time to serve the first course?

Jesus nodded to me.

I lifted the platter and made my way to the head of the table. Vinegar and wine, roasted lamb and bitter bits of *karpas*, a sour-sweet paste and a stack of bread. The scents swirled around me, and for a moment, the slaves who celebrated the first Passover in Egypt didn't seem that far away. One by one, the men at the table dabbled the bitter herbs into a cup of vinegar and swallowed the bitterness of our bondage.

Jesus lifted the wineskin from the platter, and I retreated to a darkened corner. As Jesus poured the crimson liquid into a large cup, the disciple called John asked the familiar questions:

"Why is this night different from all other nights? On all other nights we eat leavened or unleavened bread; on this night we eat only unleavened bread. On all other nights we eat all sorts of herbs; on this night we eat only bitter herbs. On all other nights we eat meat roasted, stewed, or boiled; on this night we eat only roasted meat. Why is this night different from all other nights?"[5]

Jesus was silent for a moment as he stared into his cup of wine and water, as if he noticed something in the crimson liquid to which the rest of us were blind.

Finally, he began to repeat the familiar story:

"My father was a wandering Aramean. He went down into Egypt with meager numbers and sojourned there. There he became a great and very populous nation. The Egyptians dealt harshly with us and oppressed us. They imposed heavy labor on us. We cried to *Adonai* the God of our ancestors, and *Adonai* heard our plea and saw our plight, our pain, and our oppression. *Adonai* freed us from Egypt by a mighty hand, by an outstretched arm and awesome power, and with signs and wonders.[6]

"If the Holy One had not brought our ancestors out of Egypt, then we, our children, and our grandchildren would still be Pharaoh's slaves in Egypt."

The teacher sat up, raised his hands, and began to chant the Hallel. One by one, his disciples joined in the song:

"Who is like *Adonai* our God, enthroned on high? He sees what is below, in the heavens and the earth. He raises the poor from the dust and lifts the needy from the dung heap! He sets them alongside the great—with the great leaders of his people! Hallelujah!

"When Israel went forth from Egypt, when the house of Jacob went forth from a people whose speech was strange, Judah became his holy one and Israel became his dominion. Tremble, oh earth, at the presence of *Adonai*. Tremble in the presence of Jacob's God!"[7]

Jesus handed the cup to Judas. One by one, the men around the table drank the wine—everyone except Jesus.[8] As Jesus and his followers washed their hands, I returned the platter to the head of the table. It was time for the meal.

Jesus reached for one of the flat cakes and intoned the blessing: "You are blessed, Adonai our God—he who brings forth bread from the earth. You are blessed, Adonai our God—he who has sanctified us with his commands and commanded us concerning the eating of unleavened bread."

When the rabbi broke the piece of *matzoh*, his chin fell to his chest and a moan escaped his lips, as if someone had suddenly struck him. I barely heard him murmur, "Truly, I tell you ... one of you ... will ... hand me over ... to them."

"No!" Simon jumped to his feet. "Never!"

The others at the table echoed Simon's cry.

"Surely not I!"

John whispered something in the teacher's ear. I couldn't hear Jesus' reply, but when he stood up, the room turned deathly quiet. Jesus dipped a broken bit of bread with a piece of bitter herb into the bowl of crushed figs, nuts, and vinegar. He handed the bread, still dripping with *charoset* paste, to Judas and said softly, "Do quickly what you are going to do."

Silence.

Judas grabbed his sandals and lunged toward the door. He clutched the bloodstained doorpost for a few moments before running down the steps and into the night. The piece of bread was still clenched in his fist. He never stopped to put on his sandals.

What had just happened? I was only the serving boy, but I wasn't alone in my wondering—no one present seemed certain about what had just taken place. Perhaps that's why everyone ate in such silence. The meal, the washing of the hands, the pouring of the third cup of wine.... If anyone spoke, it was in a whisper. When the last bit of flesh had been torn from the bones of the lamb, Jesus broke the silence. He began to recite the next portion of the Seder,[9] the *Birkat Ha-Mazon*:

"This is the bread of affliction that our ancestors ate when they came out of Egypt.

"You are blessed, *Adonai* our God, king of the universe—he who, in his goodness, feeds the whole world with grace, kindness, and mercy. He gives food to all flesh, for his kindness is everlasting. You are blessed, *Adonai*—he who provides food for all.

"We thank you, *Adonai* our God, for having given to our ancestors a heritage—a precious, good, and spacious land; for having brought us out, *Adonai* our God, from the land of Egypt and redeemed us from the house of slavery; for your covenant which you have sealed in our flesh; for your Torah which you have taught us; for your statutes which you have revealed to us; for the life, favor, and kindness which you have graciously given to us; and for the food we eat with which you constantly feed and sustain us every day, at all times, and at every hour.

"Our God and the God of our ancestors, may there rise and come and approach and be seen, accepted, heard, recollected, and remembered, the remembrance of us and the recollection of us, and the remembrance of our ancestors, and the remembrance of the Messiah, the descendant of David your servant, and the remembrance of Jerusalem, your holy city, and the remembrance of all your people, the house of Israel. May their remembrance come before you for life and for peace on this Feast of Unleavened Bread."

The rabbi grasped the last piece of bread and ripped the bread into two jagged chunks.

Were those drops of sweat that I saw, glistening like tiny stars beneath his eyes? Or were they tears?

"Take it, eat it," he commanded. "This is my body, broken for you. Do this in remembrance of me." John tore off a small piece and looked upward, his eyes full of questions that he did not know how to ask. The rabbi nodded. John placed the piece of bread on his tongue and passed the chunk to James. Each disciple broke a piece of bread from the chunk and chewed it, but no one seemed to know why.

Jesus raised the third cup of wine—the cup that commemorated our redemption from Egypt—and spoke the familiar blessing: "You are blessed, *Adonai*—he who created the fruit of the vine."

The cup of wine shook slightly in his hands.

He spoke in short, ragged bursts: "Drink from it, all of you. This is my blood—my blood of the new covenant—that is spilled out for many for the forgiveness of sins. I tell you this: I will not have an opportunity to drink the fruit of the vine again—not until the day when I drink it new with you in my Abba's kingdom. Do this, every time you drink it, in remembrance of me." The disciples sipped the warm wine, slowly, tentatively, uncertainly.

On every other Passover night, we laughed and sang at the end of the meal.

But on this night, everyone was silent.[10]

A Night of Memories

What made the Passover so special?

It certainly wasn't the quality of the food. If you happened to receive an ancient Passover platter in a restaurant, you'd probably send it back to the kitchen before the second bite. The vegetables were bitter, the bread was bland, the only condiment was sour wine, and the rapidly roasted meat was frequently rare and rarely tender.

What made the Passover special wasn't the meal—it was the memory. It was as if, once each year, God sat down at the table with his people, opened a tattered scrapbook, and recounted the story of his relationship with them: "See that whiskered Aramean, staring over the horizon? He was a wandering man—no one ever could get him to settle in one place for very long—but I turned him into a mighty nation. He was your ancestor. Don't forget about him.

"Here's a postcard with an Egyptian postmark. It's from the time when your people were slaves. They begged me to save them. So when the time was right, I rolled up my sleeves and rescued them. If I hadn't brought your ancestors out of Egypt, you'd be on the night shift right now, making bricks. Don't forget about them.

"Oh, and look at this picture! See the blood around the doors? That's from the night that every firstborn Egyptian died, but the angel of death passed over all the Hebrew households. That was the night when there wasn't time to leaven the bread or boil the lamb—you knew that God was going to rescue you, so you had to be ready to leave. Don't forget that evening."

The primary prayer of the Passover, the Birkat Ha-Mazon, picked up on the theme of remembering. The last lines of the prayer went something like this:

Our God and the God of our ancestors, may there ... be seen, accepted, heard, recollected, and remembered, the remembrance of us and the recollection of us, and the remembrance of our ancestors, and the remembrance of the Messiah ... and the remembrance of Jerusalem, your holy city, and the remembrance of all your people, the house of Israel. May their remembrance come before you for life and for peace on this Feast of Unleavened Bread.

In this prayer God's people were saying, "Oh, God, don't forget the story we share. Remember the covenant you made with our ancestors. Remember to send the Messiah. Remember the holy city. And, most of all, please remember *us*."

And God did.

I don't think it's a coincidence that the next command spoken by Jesus after he prayed the Birkat Ha-Mazon at the Last Supper was, "Do this in remembrance of me."[11] It was as if God was telling his disciples, "Not only did I remember my promise to your ancestors—I made a new promise and signed it in my own blood. Not only did I remember to send the Messiah—I *became* the Messiah. Not only did I remember the holy city—I am turning *you* into a holy city.[12] I have remembered you. Now, you remember me."

So we do.

It's Not About the Meal, It's About the Memory

Each day, millions of Christians throughout the world commemorate Passover. Some call it Mass, others call it Communion. Some share a common loaf, others eat wafers. Some sip from a common cup, others drink from tiny glasses that look like transparent thimbles.

Why do so many people keep returning to the Lord's Table week after week? In order to commemorate and remember the God who has chosen never to forget us. "I will not forget you," he promised his people. "Look, I have inscribed you on the palms of my hands" (Is 49:16).

In Jesus Christ, God fulfilled that promise. God promised never to forget his people, and his promise has been engraved in heaven—not in the splendor of silver and gold, but in the frailty of human flesh.

God the Son has carved the memory of us in his own body: in the crimson craters that mar his feet and hands, in the gaping hole in his side, in the ragged gashes that crisscross his back, in the scars that still crown his skull.

No longer do we need to pray, "may there ... be seen, accepted, heard, recollected, and remembered, the remembrance of us." We *have* been remembered, once and for all. That's what Holy Communion celebrates. It's not about the dry bread that sticks in our throats or the purple-tinged drink that stains our clothes. It's about the God who has chosen to remember us through the Body and Blood of his only son, Jesus Christ.

Ever feel like God has forgotten you?

Look at the bread and the wine.

See his blood in the cup?

See his scars in the loaf?

He *can't* forget you.

——A Meditation——

My Savior,
"Remember me
   when you enter your kingdom."
That's what the felon beside you asked.

Had he celebrated the Passover only a few hours earlier?
Did he remember the prayers that he had prayed?
Had he entreated *Adonai* to remember Israel?
Did he know that when he turned his head
   and saw your broken body,
      he was seeing God's answer to his prayer?
Is that why you replied,
   "Today, you will be with me in Paradise"?
You didn't look like much of an answer to prayer.
   But you were.

Thank you, my bruised and broken Savior,
   for engraving the memory of me
      in the palms of your hands,
         in the bones of your feet,
            in the hollow in your side,
               in the crown of your skull,
                  in your pierced, sacred heart.

Thank you, my Savior,
   for remembering me.
Amen.

[Jesus] looked up to heaven and said, "Father, the hour has come; glorify your Son so that the Son may glorify you, since you have given him authority over all people, to give eternal life to all whom you have given him. And this is eternal life, that they may know you, the only true God, and Jesus Christ whom you have sent. I glorified you on earth by finishing the work that you gave me to do. So now, Father, glorify me in your own presence with the glory that I had in your presence before the world existed.

"I have made your name known to those whom you gave me from the world. They were yours, and you gave them to me, and they have kept your word. Now they know that everything you have given me is from you; for the words that you gave to me I have given to them, and they have received them and know in truth that I came from you; and they have believed that you sent me.

"I am asking on their behalf; I am not asking on behalf of the world, but on behalf of those whom you gave me, because they are yours. All mine are yours, and yours are mine; and I have been glorified in them. And now I am no longer in the world, but they are in the world, and I am coming to you. Holy Father, protect them in your name that you have given me, so that they may be one, as we are one. While I was with them, I protected them in your name that you have given me.

I guarded them, and not one of them was lost except the one destined to be lost, so that the scripture might be fulfilled....

"I ask not only on behalf of these, but also on behalf of those who will believe in me through their word, that they may all be one. As you, Father, are in me and I am in you, may they also be in us, so that the world may believe that you have sent me. The glory that you have given me I have given them, so that they may be one, as we are one, I in them and you in me, that they may become completely one, so that the world may know that you have sent me and have loved them even as you have loved me. Father, I desire that those also, whom you have given me, may be with me where I am, to see my glory, which you have given me because you loved me before the foundation of the world.

"Righteous Father, the world does not know you, but I know you; and these know that you have sent me. I made your name known to them, and I will make it known, so that the love with which you have loved me may be in them, and I in them."

After Jesus had spoken these words, he went out with his disciples across the Kidron valley to a place where there was a garden, which he and his disciples entered .... and he said to his disciples, "Sit here while I go over there and pray."

From JOHN 17:1-12, 17:20-18:1; MATTHEW 26:36, NRSV

CHAPTER EIGHT

One God, One People:
The Prayer for Unity

The streets along the southern wall of Jerusalem were deserted and dark.

The faces in the torchlight were clenched like fists. Eyes wondering and wide. Skin clammy and cold. Feet stumbling occasionally in the fading sunlight.

"First, I left the Father and arrived in the world." Jesus spoke softly to avoid attracting the attention of the Roman auxiliaries who were roaming the streets that night. "Now I leave the world and travel to the Father."[1]

"Finally!" James said. "You're giving it to us straight, in plain talk—no more figures of speech. Now we know that you know everything—it all comes together in you."

"You won't have to put up with our questions anymore." Simon's tone was confident. "We're convinced that you came from God."

Jesus whirled abruptly, eyes flashing, "Do you finally believe? In fact, you're about to make a run for it—saving your own skins and abandoning me! But I'm not abandoned," he whispered. "The Father is with me."

The rabbi turned and continued walking. When his followers caught up with him, he told them, "I've told you all this so that, trusting me, you will be unshakable and assured, deeply at peace. In this godless world you will continue to experience difficulties. But take heart! I've conquered the world."

When they reached the Ashpot Gate, Jesus stopped and looked upward. His eyes closed and his face crinkled slightly. "Father," he said, "it's time. Display the bright splendor of your Son so the Son in turn may show your bright splendor. You put him in charge of everything human so he might give real and eternal life to all in his charge. And this is the real and eternal life: That they know you, the one and only true God, and Jesus Christ, whom you sent. I glorified you on earth by completing down to the last detail what you assigned me to do. And, now, Father, glorify me with your very own splendor, the very splendor I had in your presence before there was a world....

"Now I'm returning to you. I'm saying these things in the world's hearing so my people can experience my joy completed in them. I gave them your word; the godless world hated them because of it, because they didn't join the world's ways, just as I didn't join the world's ways" (Jn 17:1-16, THE MESSAGE).

Jesus slipped through the Ashpot Gate and turned toward the Mount of Olives. His disciples traipsed behind him, straining to hear, longing for a clue to help them understand what was happening.

"I'm praying not only for them but also for those who will believe in me because of them and their witness about me. The goal is for all of them to become one heart and mind—just as you, Father, are in me and I in you, so they might be one heart and mind with us. Then the world might believe that you, in fact, sent me. The same glory you gave me, I gave them, so they'll be as unified and together as we are—I in them and you in me. Then they'll be mature in this oneness, and give the godless world evidence that you've sent me and loved them in the same way you've loved me."

"Father, I want those you gave me to be with me, right where I am, so they can see my glory, the splendor you gave me, having loved me long before there ever was a world.

"Righteous Father, the world has never known you, but I have known you, and these disciples know that you sent me on this mission. I have made your very being known to them—who you are and what you do—and continue to make it known, so that your love for me might be in them exactly as I am in them" (Jn 17:17-26, THE MESSAGE).

The band of twelve trickled down the western slope of the Kidron Valley. The walls of Jerusalem loomed behind them, tossing dark shadows across the Mount of Olives.

Jesus glanced to his left. Did anyone else notice the row of torches winding toward them, slipping from the temple courts like a long, luminous serpent?

Jesus knew who stood at the head of the serpent. Only a few hours earlier, he'd washed the man's feet. Were they still clean?

The serpent continued to slither toward the Mount of Olives....
There was so little time.

A View Like None Other

Buried in the highlands of Scotland is a forested valley called Balquidder. In the ninth century, a monk named Angus glimpsed this lush, meandering depression in the earth. Overwhelmed by its breathtaking beauty, he declared it "a thin place"—a place where the separation between this world and the next was almost transparent.[2]

Thin places.... You've encountered them too.

In the watery wonder of baptism.

In the gurgling cry of a newborn baby.

In the echo of the minister's recitation, "Do this in remembrance of me."

In a sunset too beautiful to be explained by any science textbook.

All of them, thin places ... places where heaven and earth don't seem that far apart.

Jesus' prayer for unity as he made his way across the Kidron Valley is also a thin place. Through this prayer, we gain a tiny, glimmering hint of the inner splendor of God. And what we see at the center of God's being is not blinding light or raw power but a glorious relationship. We see not simply how God relates to us but how the Father, Son, and Spirit relate to one another. Remember Jesus' words?

> Now, Father, glorify me with ... the very splendor I had in
> your presence before there was a world.... I want those whom
> you gave me ... to see my glory, the splendor you gave me,
> having loved me long before there ever was a world.
>
> JOHN 17:5, 24

Long before God burst into time through the birth canal of a Jewish peasant, God the Father and God the Son played soccer with the planets, danced with God the Spirit, and simply, eternally, enjoyed the experience of being *God.* Through the thinness of this prayer, we glimpse the infinite, inner fellowship of God.

And we glimpse something else through this thin place—a profound longing within the deepest part of God to see his glorious love-relationship reflected among his people. Three times, Jesus prayed for the unity of his followers:

"Holy Father, guard them ... so they can be one heart and mind as we are one heart and mind" (Jn 17:11).

"The goal is for all of them to become one heart and mind— just as you, Father, are in me and I in you, so they might be one heart and mind with us" (Jn 17:20-21).

"The same glory you gave me, I gave them, so they'll be as unified and together as we are—I in them and you in me. Then they'll be mature in this oneness" (Jn 17:22).

"One heart and mind." "Unified and together." "Mature in this oneness." Two thousand years after Jesus prayed this prayer, we see scant evidence that any of these pleas is being answered. Denominations divide over dogma, congregations draw lines based on social demographics, and individual Christians ignore the longing for unity that flows from the inner life of God. What we have forgotten is the same simple fact the earliest Christians forgot more than once—*we need one another.*

I Need You, You Need Me

Notice the plural pronouns of Jesus' prayer:

"I gave *them* your word."

"The same glory you gave me, I gave *them.*"

"I have made your very being known to *them* ... so that your love for me might be in *them* exactly as I am in *them.*"

Not once in this prayer did Jesus declare, "I gave *her* your word," or "the same glory you gave to me, I gave to *him.*" Just as in the Lord's Prayer, the context for the Christian faith is not the experience of a lone individual. The Christian faith requires a community of fellow believers. It is neither "I" nor "me," neither "him" nor "her"; it is always "we" and "us," "they" and "them."

If I take this prayer for unity seriously, I must give up the arrogant illusion that my salvation, my spiritual life, and my sins are personal matters. I must admit that I cannot follow Jesus Christ alone any more than I can get married alone. To follow Jesus, I need the fellowship of other believers. So do you, and so has every saint in the history of the church.

> Christianity is inherently communal, a matter of life in the Body, the church. Jesus did not call isolated individuals to follow him. He called a group of disciples. He gathered a crowd.
>
> Privacy is not a Christian category. We are saved from our privacy by being made part of a people who can tell us what we should do with our money, with our genitals, with our lives. We have been made part of a good company, a wonderful adventure, so that we no longer need "mine."[3]

That's why it's not completely accurate to say that any of us has a "personal relationship with Jesus." What we have is a *communal* relationship with Jesus. I owe my understanding of Jesus Christ to the scribes who preserved the stories, the saints who lived the stories, and the Sunday school teachers who repeated the stories even when I was more concerned with impressing the female class members with my belching abilities. (I set the class record, by the way—nine seconds, no pauses, while reciting the opening lines of the Declaration of Independence. The founding fathers would have been proud.)

Were these scribes and saints and Sunday school teachers perfect? No, they were as imperfect as the men and women who share your pew every Sunday morning. The scribes made some mistakes, the saints sinned, and by the end of our class time, my Sunday school teacher was inexplicably cranky. But I needed every one of them.

Without the scribes, I could never have experienced the raw honesty of the prophet Jeremiah or the concern for the downtrodden that has led me to love Luke's Gospel. Without the diverse saints of the past and present, my faith in Jesus Christ would never have grown beyond the simple plea of a five-year-old boy: "I need to know Jesus."

"The Miraculously Mismatched Community"

That's why I have no desire to join a church filled with people "just like me." If everyone's educational level, economic status, and racial profile were similar to mine, why would we need each other? Part of the "foolishness of the cross" is the fact that those who rub shoulders in the shadow of the cross are people whom the world would never dream of blending together (see 1 Cor 1:18, 26).

When I gather to worship and to pray with my Christian family, I long to be surrounded by a congregation that's as multicultural as an Eskimo drinking kosher vodka from a Mason jar. I want to sing the *Gloria Patri* back-to-back with "We Shall Overcome," "I'll Fly Away," and a string of rollicking praise choruses. I want to shake brown hands and white hands, smooth hands and callused hands, wrinkled hands and tiny, trembling, newborn hands.

Why? Because church is not about my personal tastes or desires. In fact, church is not about *me* at all. It is about a mismatched community of recovering sinners, bound by a Spirit that no one has ever seen. C.S. Lewis wrote that in the first few weeks after becoming a Christian,

I thought that I could do it on my own, by retiring to my room and reading theology.... I disliked very much [the hymns that they sang in church], which I considered to be fifth-rate poems set to sixth-rate music. But as I went on, I saw the great merit of it. I came up against different people of quite different outlooks and different education, and then gradually my conceit just began peeling off. I realized that the hymns ... were, nevertheless, being sung with devotion and benefit by an old saint in elastic-side boots in the opposite pew, and then you realize that you aren't fit to clean those boots. It gets you out of your solitary conceit.[4]

To share "one heart and mind" with our fellow-believers means that we will give up our foolish delusion that we can make it on our own. We confess this surrender of self-centeredness in the Apostles' Creed by declaring, "I believe in the *communion of the saints*." And, as I contemplate the crazy collection of believers that repeats the ancient creed alongside me, my own mind echoes, "I believe in *this* communion of saints—for without you, I could not believe at all. I believe in *this* communion of saints—for this fellowship is the sphere of the Spirit's work in my life. I believe in *this* communion of saints—for you are my sacrament, the living reflection of the body and blood of Jesus, broken for me." Walter Burkhardt, a Jesuit writer, put it this way:

I love this church, this living, pulsing, sinning People of God.... Why? For all the Christian hate, I experience here a community of love. For all the institutional idiocy, I find here a tradition of reason.... For all the fear of sex, I discover here the redemption of my body. In an age so inhuman, I touch here tears of compassion. In a world so grim and humorless, I share here rich joy and earthy laughter. In the midst of death, I hear an incomparable stress on life. For all the apparent absence of God, I sense here the real presence of Christ.[5]

The Reason to Believe

The community of faith has a greater function than my personal spiritual development, though. Jesus Christ left only one proof that he had spoken the truth. It wasn't logically sound—in fact, it wasn't logical at all. It was the unity of his people. According to his prayer, "The goal is for all of them to become one heart and mind.... Then the world might believe that you, in fact, sent me.... They'll ... give the godless world evidence that you've sent me" (Jn 17:20-22, THE MESSAGE).

Did you get what Jesus was saying? Let me paraphrase his point: *The world will be won not through the wisdom of our words but through the witness of our oneness.*

I know, I know. It sounds pretty crazy to me too. Someone once commented that the communion of saints is a lot like Noah's ark—if it weren't for the storm on the outside, no one could stand the fact that it smells like you-know-what on the inside. But what would happen if we focused less on the church's shortcomings and more on the church's wondrous possibilities? While I don't see the unification of all of God's people anywhere on the immediate horizon, I do believe that every Christian could demonstrate to the world a *spirit* of unity.

According to Jesus, our best hope for convincing the world that he was no ordinary human being is our unity (see Jn 17:21). For only then do we accurately reflect the inner nature of God—a nature in which the diversity of Father, Son, and Spirit coexist in perfect complementarity.

Suppose that we did constantly consider the fact that the way we commune with our fellow believers is the primary proof of God's presence in Jesus Christ. (If, after all, God's power can't change your prejudices and mine, can persons outside the Christian faith really expect him to change their lives?) Perhaps then the world would see that despite its many failures, the church *is* a wondrous miracle. It is loving and forgiving, laughing and weeping, worshiping and seeking God in the midst of this motley multitude of sinners and saints.

What Was in That Cup?

Immediately after Jesus prayed for the unity of his people, he entered into the Garden of Gethsemane. Remember the scene?

> Jesus said to them, "I'm deeply distressed, to the point of death...." He went a little farther, then he threw himself on the ground. He prayed that, if possible, the hour might pass him by. He said, "Abba! Father! Everything is possible for you. Remove this cup from me. And, yet, don't do what I want. Do what you want."
>
> MARK 14:34–36

I wonder, was Jesus' sorrow only the distress of the agony that he would soon face? Or did he, perhaps, look forward in time and glimpse our disunity? Was that part of his pain? Did he witness the controversies and the crusades that would shatter his body into thousands of sects? Did he hear the backbiting and the bitterness that besmirches the fellowship in your church and in mine?

I don't know.

But I do know this: Even if he didn't witness our disunity in the garden, he bore it on the cross. For our disunity is sin.

Do we want the world to believe in Christ? Philosophical apologetics are easier. Witnessing manuals are cheaper. But neither one provides the proof for which Christ prayed: "The goal is for all of them to become one ... so the world will believe that you sent me."

The Thin Place

Want to experience the ultimate thin place—a place where heaven and earth intersect?

How about a unified church? (The world would *never* be able to explain away that one.)

Not certain where to begin? (I mean, getting the Orthodox and Catholic Churches back together *might* be a little too ambitious a project for this weekend.)

How about asking that church member you can't stand to eat lunch with you on Sunday?

Hey, I never said it would be easy.

——A MEDITATION——

Lord of all creation and Lord of the church,
   It's easy to love the church.
It's not so easy to love certain members of the church.
You prayed to your Father,
   "I want them to be one even as we are one."
You commanded your first followers,
   "Love one another, just as I have loved you."

Did you really mean it?
Are you sure?
 No exceptions?
      Everyone?
            Even ... you-know-who?
Could it be that your words were a promise *and* a command?
When you commanded, "Love one another,"
   were you also promising,
      "You *will be able* to love one another"?
When you prayed, "I want them to be one,"
   were you also promising,
      "They *will be able* to be one"?
   I hope so.
Help me to see that I cannot honestly love your church—
   or *you*—
      unless I also love the members of your church.
         Even ... you-know-who.
God, be merciful to me, a sinner—
this could take a while.
Amen.[6]

IV.

KNOWING THE GOD WHO CREATES A NEW FUTURE

Three truths—each one embedded in a prayer.
  God suffers with us—
    "My God! My God! Why have you forsaken me?"
  God's favor rests upon us—
    "May the Lord make his face to shine upon you."
  God's glory is present in us—
    "The glory that you have given me I have given them."

Three truths that form a new future
  for those who call God "Abba"—
    a future with a God
        who comprehends his children's sorrows,
        who shines on his children's lives,
        who transforms his children to reflect
            the infinite glory
            of his Son.

Then Jesus said, "Father, forgive them; for they do not know what they are doing." And they cast lots to divide his clothing.

From noon on, darkness came over the whole land until three in the afternoon. And about three o'clock Jesus cried with a loud voice, *"Eli, Eli, lema sabachthani?"* that is, "My God, my God, why have you forsaken me?" When some of the bystanders heard it, they said, "This man is calling for Elijah."

After this, when Jesus knew that all was now finished, he said (in order to fulfill the scripture), "I am thirsty." A jar full of sour wine was standing there. So they put a sponge full of the wine on a branch of hyssop and held it to his mouth.... Jesus said, "Father, into your hands I commend my spirit." Then, crying with a loud voice, he said, "It is finished." Having said this, he breathed his last.

From Matthew 27:45–47; Luke 23:34–35, 46; John 19:28–30, NRSV

CHAPTER NINE

Praying in the Darkness:
The Prayers of the Cross

Darkness.

Like a vast, black cloak unfolding in the eastern sky.

Darkness at noonday.[1]

Hollow, aching shadows, washing over the land until the hills become indistinct.

Formless.

Formless and void. As if God has hurled the cosmos back to the beginning and started over.

A whisper, from the crest of the hill: "Abba, forgive them. They don't know what they are doing."

A woman stands silently on the slope.[2] Despite the cluster of bodies around her, she stands alone in her sorrow. It isn't the first time. Only years of heartache can plow furrows in a woman's face like the ones that crisscross her forehead.

Mary can no longer see the sun or moon. Every luminous sphere seems to have slipped from the sky and drowned in the Great Sea. The only light is the horrible, haunting glow that smolders along the distant horizon. Still, it is enough, just enough to see her son.

Naked. Dangling from iron spikes. Mangled, his gaping gashes covered with flies and congealed blood. His skull crudely crowned with a thorn bush.[3] His robe—the robe that her hands had woven for him—

now draped across the shoulders of a Roman auxiliary who stands at the crest of the hill.

The words of the white-robed messenger still echo in the recesses of Mary's heart: "He will be great! He will rule the house of Jacob forever! His kingdom will never end." Perhaps he had been great, but he had never ruled a kingdom. He'd never even wanted one, it seemed. Yet she had never stopped hoping.

Until this morning. Until John Bar-Zebedee screamed her name from the courtyard of the house in Bethany. Until she and John staggered up the Hill of the Skull and she glimpsed her son, spread-eagled beneath the sneering words on the placard nailed above him: "King of the Jews." If he is a king, his is a pathetic kingdom. His only throne is a bloody stake, stabbed into the Hill of the Skull, and his only soldier is an unarmed fisherman surrounded by a mob of sobbing women.

Mary opens her eyes and sees nothing. Utter blackness has descended like a starving vulture, devouring every glimmer of light. How long has she stood in this darkness? Minutes or hours? She cannot tell. Time has ceased. Only infinite, empty blackness remains.

"Eli!" a ragged shriek rips the silent void. "Eli! Lema sabachthani?"

A cry like no one has heard before.

A cry from the depths of hell.

A voice that the woman at the cross knows too well.

The voice of her son.

"My God! My God! Why have you abandoned me?"

The woman crumples to the ground, retching, longing to expel the anguish that has torn her stomach in two. Too much ... too much ... it is too much. To the Jewish leaders, her son has been a nuisance, healing lepers one moment and hobnobbing with prostitutes the next. To the Romans, he has been a threat—Jews from Galilee had an annoying habit of turning into violent revolutionaries. But to the woman on the hill, this man was always the flailing infant who suckled his life from her breast ... the curly-haired toddler with the splinter in his palm ... the boy whom she loved so deeply but who never truly belonged to her ... the young man who wandered out of the carpentry shop one morning and never came back. Now he dangled from a splintered beam, his skin shredded by the whip, his wrists shattered by iron spikes, his dark, brooding eyes swollen and bruised.

The elderly priest in the temple had warned her: "A sword will pierce your own heart." But she had never imagined that this would be part of the deal. "Dear God of my fathers," she moans, "what went wrong? How could I have saved him?"

When she raises her head, hints of sunlight are frolicking unevenly along the horizon, mocking her pain. One by one, jagged streaks of crimson and orange emerge until the western sky seems to be on fire, like the end of time—or was it the beginning?

Mary barely hears her son's request: "I ... thirst." A bystander plunges a grimy sponge into the Roman soldier's jug of posca. He mounts the sponge on a branch and rams it into Jesus' face. The Galilean strains forward and gnaws the sponge desperately, drawing the acrid liquid into his swollen throat.[4]

Suddenly, Jesus looks up, beyond Mary, beyond the Holy City, as if he is searching for a certain, familiar face that has eluded him for too long.

"Abba ..." Bloodied lips struggle to form the word. "Abba ... into your hands I give my spirit."

Without warning, his body twists upward, enabling him to inhale sharply. The final words of Jesus tear across the landscape like a lion's roar.

"It ...

... is ...

... finished!"

His head slumps forward against his chest.

Silence sweeps the Hill of the Skull.

Mary feels her legs pulling her up the slope. She is running. At the crest of the hill, she collapses, pummeling the wooden stake with her fists as she tumbles to the ground. Her fingertips rake and gouge the moist earth.

No words can express her sorrow. No tears are left to drown it. All that remains is utter, aching emptiness. She lies in the dirt, heaving, unable to move. At last, a mantle falls gently across her shoulders, and tender hands lift her to her feet. "Mother," she hears a distant murmur, "my dear mother, it's your son, John. Let's go home."

Holiness in the Midst of Unholiness

In the opening scene of the film *La Dolce Vita,* a helicopter hovers above the meadows of central Italy. The statue of a man swings gently beneath the helicopter. His arms are open wide, as if he longs to embrace the lush landscape that passes underneath his feet. His head is slightly bowed, as if he is preparing to pray. The helicopter drifts across a freshly plowed field, and several farmers recognize the robed figure.

"Jesus!" one farmhand cries. "It's Jesus!"

When the helicopter reaches the outskirts of Rome, the pilot glimpses several bikini-clad beauties relaxing beside a pool. The helicopter circles abruptly and hovers above the pool. The workers in the aircraft strain to look past the statue, to gain a better view of the women beneath them.

For a few moments, the Lord Jesus Christ hovers above the pool, arms outspread and head bowed. The sacred statue seems strangely out of place. Jesus doesn't belong here. And yet here he is—an unexpected outburst of holiness in the midst of an unholy event.

The same could be said for the prayers that Jesus prayed from the cross. They were unexpected outbursts of holiness in the midst of human selfishness and sin. They were as out of place on a cross as was the statue of the Savior dangling above the shapely citizens of some picturesque Italian suburb.

Jesus wasn't the first Jewish revolutionary the Roman soldiers had hammered to the splintered crossbeams. The soldiers knew precisely what to expect from this brand of criminal. Before the ill-fated Galilean lapsed into delirium, he would pray at least two prayers. One prayer would be a curse, the other would be a confession.

But this wonder-working radical from Nazareth was different from the others.

Instead of the curse, he requested forgiveness—not for himself but for the soldiers who had spat upon him, for the bystanders who mocked him, for the centurion whose cold spear would find its way into his side. And instead of a confession, he begged heaven for an answer. Heaven never yielded an audible reply, but that didn't stop a centurion from whispering, "Surely, this one must have been innocent" (Lk 23:47). Never before had he encountered a man like this— a man who never cursed, who never confessed, and who never gave up.

The First Prayer From the Cross: The Plea of Forgiveness

Let's be brutally honest for a moment: Cursing can bring a sense of satisfaction. I don't mean using colorful language. By "cursing," I mean asking God to give someone what he deserves. The whole idea is a bit self-righteous—after all, if God gave everyone what she or he deserved, I wouldn't be around to write these words and you wouldn't have survived long enough to read them. And yet, this sort of cursing appears throughout the Hebrew Scriptures.

King David pleaded, "Oh Lord, let my enemies be put to shame!"

(Ps 13:2; 109:28). Jeremiah, the so-called weeping prophet, spent more time cursing than he did crying. "Oh Lord," he prayed once, "Don't ever pardon my enemies' sins. Cause them to fall on their faces. Deal with them on the day when you are most angry!" (Jer 18:23; 15:15; 17:18; 20:12). When King Joash's minions murdered one of his priests, the priest bellowed, "May the Lord see this and avenge me!" (2 Chr 24:22).

The soldiers around the cross of Christ expected this self-proclaimed Messiah to follow the tradition of his ancestors. After all, curses were what they had heard from every other Jewish rabble-rouser. And it wasn't as if Jesus hadn't cursed anyone before. Pharisees, fig trees, entire cities—Jesus had cursed them all at least once. Sometimes, his curses had been as colorful as Jeremiah's: "Wretchedness upon you, scribes and Pharisees! You two-faced people! You cross sea and land to convert one person—then you make that convert twice the spawn of hell that you already are" (Mt 23:15). Jesus had even cursed one of his own disciples: "Wretchedness upon the one who betrays the Son of humanity! It would have been better for that one if he had never been born!" (Mt 26:24).

Yet, on the cross, Jesus cursed no one. Not the disciples who had high-tailed it out of the garden as soon as they saw the warrant for their teacher's arrest. Not the soldiers who had found amusement in the beating of a helpless prisoner. Not even the auxiliary who had hammered a spike through his wrist. Why? The apostle Paul recorded the answer: "Christ released us from the curse of the Law by *becoming the curse for us*" (Gal 3:13, emphasis mine).

Why didn't the crucified Christ curse anyone?

Because on the cross, he *became* the curse.

He did not curse because he *was* the curse.

Jesus Christ did not scream at the sneering spectators, "May God deal with your sin on the day when he is most angry!"—the punishment for their sacrilege was already consuming his own inmost being. He did not cry to the Roman auxiliaries, "Wretchedness upon you!"— his own soul was already choking on the wretchedness of their sin. He did not even whisper, "Oh Lord, put my enemies to shame"—for in that moment, he *became* the enemy of God. On the cross Jesus did not merely bear the pain of God's punishment for sin—he *became* the pain, the shame, the curse of humanity's sin.

That's why the soldiers never heard the curse they anticipated. Instead, they heard an utterly unexpected outburst of holiness in the midst of this unholy event: "Father, forgive them; for they do not know what they are doing" (Lk 23:34). Jesus could forgive them instead of cursing them because he had taken the curse of their sin and made it his own.

At times I would prefer to ignore the first prayer from the cross. I don't know about the people who cross your path, but the people in my life sometimes deserve a curse or two in the tradition of David, Jeremiah, and Zechariah. I have met deacons who are dishonest and youth who are disrespectful. The other drivers on the highway are disagreeable, and the waitress forgot to put a slice of lemon in my Diet Coke *again*. And me? Well, honestly, I'm no better than any of them. Yet if I believe that Jesus Christ became the curse of God, I cannot pray, "Oh Lord, give them what they deserve." What I must pray instead is, "Father, forgive them. Maybe they know what they're doing, maybe they don't. It doesn't really matter. What matters is that your Son became the curse that they deserve. I bear nothing, for you have already borne it all." Hopefully, they are willing to say the same about me.

While cursing in the tradition of the prophets may seem more satisfying—at least for the first few moments—human curses will always ring hollow in the ears of those who have taken their stand in the shadow of the cross. So I forgive the deacons, I love the youth, and I smile at the reckless cretin in the black S.U.V. And the waitress? I give her a 20 percent tip anyway. The central image of the Christian faith is, after all, a cross—not a set of scales. If the central image of the faith *were* a set of scales, *I* would have been the one on the cross.

The Second Prayer From the Cross: The Cry for an Answer

Decades of Jewish tradition had provided a prayer for nearly every life experience, from the washing of hands to the sighting of a rainbow. There was even a prayer for the experience of being executed. It was a simple plea: "May my death atone for all my sins."[5] The Roman soldiers had probably never seen a Jewish victim of crucifixion go to his grave without murmuring some variation of this confession—not even the self-righteous messianic pretenders who sprouted like wildflowers in the Galilean hills.

Not until that Friday, on the eve of Passover. *That* Friday, when the Romans nailed the rabbi from Nazareth to the wooden beams. The Nazarene never prayed the prayer of confession. He could not, of course, because he had no sins to confess. Yet in that moment, Jesus *was* sinful. According to the apostle Paul, "God caused him who knew no sin to be sin" (2 Cor 5:21). Paul did not write, "God caused him ... to bear sin," or "to die for sin." No! God the Father caused God the Son "to *be* sin"! That is the horrible paradox of the cross: On that Friday, the Sinless One became the sinfulness of all sinners, the vile essence of sin itself. On the cross,

> Jesus becomes a bad man, the worst of all men, the badness, in fact, of all men and all women together.... Between the third hour and the ninth hour, beneath a blackening sky, Jesus becomes the rebellion of humankind against its God.... Yet this

same Jesus is also the Holy One of God.... Holy, he must hate sin with an unyielding hatred. Behold, then, and see a sorrow unlike any other sorrow in the universe: that right now Jesus hates himself with unyielding hatred.[6]

In this way, God gains a ghastly new experience: Through Jesus Christ, God experiences sin. Not the experience of committing sin. Not the fleeting rush of false satisfaction that seduces us into coming back for more. Not the feeble imitations of God's pleasure that the world foolishly calls pleasure. No, God experiences sin as it truly is: God experiences the decades of self-hatred that follow the fleeting rush of pleasure; God drinks down the darkest dregs of addiction and exploitation; God freely endures the eternal damnation for my flirtations with the boundaries of iniquity.[7] Joni Eareckson Tada poignantly describes the pain of Jesus in these moments:

> His Father! He must face his Father like this!
> From heaven the Father now rouses himself like a lion disturbed, shakes his mane, and roars against the shriveling remnant of a man hanging on a cross: "Son of Man! Why have you behaved so? You have cheated, lusted, stolen, gossiped—murdered, envied, hated, lied.... Oh, the duties you have shirked, the children you have abandoned!... What a self-righteous, pitiful drunk—*you*, who molest young boys, peddle killer drugs, travel in cliques, and mock your parents.... Does the list never end! Splitting families, raping virgins, acting smugly, playing the pimp—buying politicians, practicing extortion, filming pornography, accepting bribes.... I hate, I *loathe* these things in you! Disgust for everything about you consumes me! Can you not feel my wrath?" The Father watches as his heart's treasure, the

mirror-image of himself, sinks drowning into raw, liquid sin. Jehovah's stored wrath against humankind from every century explodes in a single direction.

"My God! My God! Why have you forsaken me?"

But heaven stops its ears. The Son stares up at the One who cannot, who will not, reach down or reply. Two eternal hearts tear—their intimate friendship shaken to the depths.[8]

In the words of the prophet Isaiah, "He was wounded for our transgressions, crushed for our iniquities; upon him was the punishment that made us whole, and by his bruises we are healed. All we like sheep have gone astray; we have all turned to our own way, and the Lord has laid on him the iniquity of us all" (Is 53:4-6). And nothing can ease his sorrow—not a prayer of confession, not the forgiveness of his Father, not even some sweet internal awareness that he is innocent. For in this moment, God the Son is sin. Yet he cannot confess his sinfulness, because his sin is not his own. This was "the cup"—the experience of God's wrath—that he begged his Father to let him bypass (see Mk 14:36; cf. Ps 11:6; 75:8).

The crowd around the cross expects a prayer of confession. What they hear instead of a confession is a cry of absolute agony: "My God! My God! Why have you abandoned me?" Jesus cannot beg, "Have mercy on me"—how can a holy God have mercy on the essence of sin? He cannot plead, "*Abba*, forgive me"—of what sin can his Father forgive him? He can only pray for an answer—"My God! My God! Why have you abandoned me?"

His cry is a quotation from one of David's psalms. But screamed from the cross, the prayer is no pious recitation of a passage from the Hebrew Scriptures. This is a cry of utter desperation. This is the cry of God the Son, utterly forsaken by his Father. The face that Moses was forbidden to see (see Ex 33:19–20) is now turned toward the heavens, screaming for an answer.

This prayer is, I believe, Christianity's only answer to the problems of pain and suffering. It's an embarrassing answer, to be sure—after all, what other religion worships a deity who was senseless enough to get himself nailed to a cross? But only a God who has dangled from a cross can empathize with his people when their circumstances nail them to crosses of loneliness, loss, abandonment, and abuse. Such a God knows how it feels to be the victim. For, on the cross, he *chose* to become the victim.

The second prayer from the cross doesn't provide us with an escape from the problems of pain and suffering. It doesn't even provide us with answers to our questions of why. What it does provide is a reminder that we never suffer alone. And maybe, in the moments when we feel abandoned by God, that's the only answer we really need—which brings us to the third prayer Jesus prayed from the cross.

The Third Prayer From the Cross: The Way of Ruthless Trust
It is almost the ninth hour. The sun is beginning to peek through the clouds again. The priests on the temple mount breathe a sigh of relief. They will be able to offer the evening sacrifice after all. The Passover lambs, already slaughtered and flayed, dangle from wooden racks in the Court of Israel. As priests scurry to remove the carcasses from the iron hooks, the high priest lifts his arms and speaks the invocation for the evening sacrifice: "Into your hands I give my spirit!" (Ps 31:5).[9]

At this moment, another man quotes the same Scripture: "Father," he prays, "into your hands I give my spirit." Through this prayer, prayed at this moment, Jesus Christ identifies himself as the Passover sacrifice. Yet what amazes me most about his prayer is the word that he adds to the quotation—*Father*. He may even have used the intimate term, Abba. God the Father has cursed him, forsaken him, and caused him to become the essence of sin, but Jesus never gives up on his Father's love. He does not merely trust his Father; he trusts his Father with what Brennan Manning has termed "*ruthless trust.*"

What is ruthless trust? It's refusing to give up on God's love for humanity, even when God seems to be playing on the wrong team. It's Jacob, putting the messenger of God in a headlock and panting, "I will not let you go until you bless me" (Gn 32:26). It's Job crying out, "Though he slay me, yet will I trust him" (Job 13:15). It's John, abandoned on the island of Patmos, still seeking the Spirit's presence on the Lord's Day (see Rv 1:1–8). It's the rural pastor, spending the best years of his ministry in a church that has broken his heart, because that's where God has placed him. It's the new parents, standing over a pink-ruffled crib, praying, "Heal her or take her—we will still praise you." It's Jesus of Nazareth gasping after six hours of agony, "*Abba,* beloved Father, into your hands I commit my spirit."

[Ruthless trust] inspires us to thank God for the spiritual darkness that envelops us, for the loss of income, for the nagging arthritis that is so painful, and to pray from the heart, "Abba, in your hands I entrust my body, mind, and spirit and this entire day…. Whatever you want of me, *I* want of me, falling into you and trusting you in the midst of my life. Into your heart, I entrust my heart, feeble, distracted, insecure, uncertain. Abba, unto you I abandon myself in Jesus our Lord. Amen."[10]

The path of ruthless trust is a difficult path, to be sure. Yet for those who follow the man on the center cross, it's the *only* path.

Reflections of God's Heart

Three prayers, spoken from the cross:

> The first a model of grace.
>
> The second a source of comfort.
>
> The last an example of trust.
>
> Each one a reflection of the heart of God.

------A MEDITATION------

Lord of creation,
  Lord of the cross,
The folk at the foot of the cross expected a curse—
  it's what I would have expected too.
      I would have told the whole lot of them to go to hell.
But you forgave them—you *forgave* them, for Christ's sake!
  No, no, it wasn't for Christ's sake, was it?
      It was for *our* sake.
      To teach us that we can do better
          than giving people what they deserve.
              We can give them mercy.
              This is your grace.
The folk at the foot of the cross expected a confession—
  it's what I would have expected too.
      Even Messiahs don't have completely clear consciences,
      do they?
But you cried for an answer—did you already know what it was?
  Perhaps you did, perhaps you didn't, I don't know.
  This I *do* know:
      It was for *our* sake.
      To teach us that because you became sin,
          we will never suffer alone again.
              God suffers with us.
              This is our comfort.
The folk at the foot of the cross expected you
to give up on your Father—
  it's what I would have expected too.
      Whenever my cross gets heavy, I want to give up.

But you still called God "Abba"—how did you do it?

How did you hold on?

It was for *our* sake, wasn't it?

To teach us the way of ruthless trust

in a heavenly Father

who will never let us go.

This is your promise.

Show me how

to share your grace,

to embrace your comfort,

to trust your promise.

Amen.

——The Priestly Benediction——

The Lord spoke to Moses, saying: "Speak to Aaron and his sons, saying, Thus you shall bless the Israelites: You shall say to them, the Lord bless you and keep you; the Lord make his face to shine upon you, and be gracious to you; the Lord lift up his countenance upon you, and give you peace. "So they shall put my name on the Israelites, and I will bless them."

Numbers 6:22–27, NRSV

Then he led them out as far as Bethany, and, lifting up his hands, he blessed them. While he was blessing them, he withdrew from them and was carried up into heaven. And they worshiped him, and returned to Jerusalem with great joy; and they were continually in the temple blessing God.

Luke 24:50–53, NRSV

CHAPTER TEN

May the Lord Make His Face to Shine Upon You: The Priestly Benediction

No one—not even John—could keep up with him. Jesus bounded up the eastern slope of the Kidron Valley toward the Mount of Olives. His feet were bare, and his hair streamed behind him like the banner of a king. All the wildness and wonder of the created order seemed to surge from his body. He ran like a man who for the first time in his life was finally free.

His mother scurried up the Mount of Olives, arm-in-arm with Mary Magdalene. Joanna and Salome, Clopas and Mary the mother of James and John, relatives and disciples—all of them trailed behind him, breathless with joy, and desperate never to let the teacher out of their sight again.

He raced through the groves of trees, past the stone olive-presses that surrounded the Garden of Gethsemane. The scents of spring swirled around him, strong and fresh in the morning air. Rays from the rising sun pierced the treetops and filled the grove with a thousand tiny shafts of light. Life seemed to erupt from the song of every sparrow, from the frightened leap of every hare, from the emerald hue of every blade of grass.

When Jesus emerged from the trees on the eastern side of the Mount of Olives, he stopped abruptly, tumbling down the slope, laughing in harmony with the morning breeze. His followers gathered around him, and he began to embrace each of them.

When he reached his mother, Mary, they laughed until they wept and then laughed some more. She clutched his arm and kissed the wounds that still marred his wrist. She didn't know how and she wasn't certain when, but the sword that had pierced her heart for so many years was gone.

When the teacher gripped Simon's shoulders, the big fisherman stiffened. His face burned with the shame of his denial, and his eyes brimmed with the guilt of his sin. He stared at the stones beneath his feet until he heard the gentle sentence, "Simon, don't forget to feed my sheep."

"Lord," Simon ventured, "is this the time when you will restore the kingdom of Israel?"

The teacher chuckled, "Simon, Simon Peter—tough as a stone, unstable as a pebble, part of the bedrock of my church." He glanced at the other disciples. "The times and the periods that the Father has set by his power are not for any of you to know. Let me tell you about the power that is for you: The Holy Spirit will fall upon you, and you will testify about me in Jerusalem, in Judea and Samaria, even into the farthest reaches of the earth" (Acts 1:7-8).

Jesus stepped away from the crowd and raised his hands. Behind him, the morning sun shone through the smoky pillars that drifted upward from newly kindled fires in the villages of Bethphage and Bethany. His mother closed her eyes in the glaring light.

When Jesus spoke, it was not merely his voice that Mary heard. A multitude of voices seemed to resound around him: "May *Adonai* bless you and keep you. May *Adonai* make his face to shine upon you and be gracious to you. May *Adonai* lift his countenance upon you and give ..."

Mary didn't hear the final words of the benediction. She opened her eyes to look into her son's face, but she could see nothing but light, blinding light. The sun had grown so bright—or was it the sun? For the briefest moment, she glimpsed the familiar outline of his body; then suddenly, she couldn't see him at all.

He was gone.

The Final Blessing

Forty days after the terror of the cross and the triumph of the empty tomb, the disciples finally saw Jesus ascend to his Father. For a few moments they stood, eyes wide and mouths sagging open, wondering what to do next. The duo of white-robed messengers didn't provide any help. "You Galileans!" they chided. "Why are you standing here, staring into the heavens? He's coming back in the same way that you saw him go" (Acts 1:11).

Yes, but when? And how? The directions that Jesus left were indefinite: "Stay here until you are clothed with power," he told them—but he never explained how they would know that their clothing had arrived (see Lk 24:49). According to Luke, "while he was blessing them, he ... was taken up into heaven" (Lk 24:51).

Ever feel like the disciples probably felt? Ever feel like God's presence has been whisked away into another realm? Like all that remains of his presence is the distant echo of his blessing? Don't despair—that distant echo of his blessing may be all you need. It was, after all, all that the disciples needed. After Jesus ascended, they "returned to Jerusalem with great joy. They were all ... blessing God" (Lk 24:52-53).

Why were they able to leave the vacant spot where Jesus had stood and dash into Jerusalem with psalms of joy ringing from their lips? I think it had to do with the blessing that he spoke as he was leaving.

The Priestly Benediction

What blessing did Jesus leave echoing in the ears of his first followers? No one can be certain, but it seems that Jesus was speaking the ancient priestly benediction when his Father welcomed him home. Notice the resemblance between the description of Aaron's priestly benediction and Luke's account of Jesus' final moments on this earth: "Aaron lifted his hands ... and blessed them. Then, he came down from the mountain" (Lv 9:22–24). "Jesus lifted his hands and blessed them. While he was blessing them,... he was taken up into the heavens" (Lk 24:51–53).[1]

If Jesus was conferring the priestly benediction, his blessing was a quotation from the book of Numbers: "May the Lord bless you and keep you. May the Lord make his face to shine upon you and be gracious to you. May the Lord lift his countenance upon you and give you peace" (Nm 6:22-27).

In the Old Testament, these words had revealed the relationship that God desired to have with the Israelites. Through this benediction, God longed to reveal his grace—"make his face to shine"—among his people. That's why this benediction became a central part of Israel's worship. The priestly benediction echoed in the temple after every act of obedience to the Torah, in the homes of Jewish children after every synagogue service, in the temple courts when Simeon blessed the infant Christ. It was the blessing through which God imprinted his sacred identity on the Israelite people (see Nm 6:26–27). And when Jesus vanished into the eastern horizon, this benediction was all the disciples had left.

The Embodied Benediction

The disciples didn't deserve the benediction. Six weeks earlier, on this same hill, they had scampered into the bushes when the soldiers showed up. During and after their rabbi's arrest, they deserted him, denied him, doubted him, and—except for a botched bit of swash-buckling swordplay, courtesy of Simon Peter—never once defended him. Yet in his final moments among them, Jesus didn't say, "Remember what happened right over there, in the Garden of Gethsemane? Don't *ever* pull a stunt like that again!" Instead, in the very spot where this fickle band of followers had failed him, Jesus asked his Father to bless them. Then, suddenly, he was gone.

And the disciples?

They were a little shocked, I suppose. Still, after Jesus was gone, "they worshiped him." It was one thing to worship Jesus while his feet were on the ground. But to worship him after he was gone was to confess that somehow he was still present among them. They still didn't know *when* Jesus would return. Neither did they know *how* they would get to the Father. But they did know—finally—*who* had revealed himself among them. They understood that the risen Christ had not simply spoken the benediction. In Jesus Christ, the benediction of God became flesh.

In Jesus Christ, God *blessed* his people by giving them the gift of himself. He *kept* those who loved him by imprinting his own identity upon their lives (see Jn 17:11-12). He *shined his face* upon his followers—not only by giving them his love,[2] but also by giving them a glimpse of his glory on the mountain, where his countenance "shone like the sun" (Mt 17:2). And he gave *grace* upon grace (see Jn 1:16) and *peace*—not peace like the world offers, but the perfect contentment of his own presence (see Jn 14:27).

In Jesus Christ, the living God blessed his people, kept them, caused his countenance to shine favorably upon them, and offered them grace and peace—forever.

By the time Jesus blessed his disciples on the Mount of Olives, the people of Israel had heard the benediction for fifteen centuries. But only in Jesus Christ did anyone *become* the benediction. The benediction that he spoke was a reminder of the benediction that he was.

Living the Benediction

Dial my telephone number and after the fourth ring, here's what you'll hear: "Hi! You've reached the home of Timothy and Rayann Jones. Even though God answers everyone who calls on him, we don't. So leave your name and your number, and we'll call you back as soon as we can." (Actually, you'll hear a shrieking guitar solo before the message—I like to make certain that you *really* want to talk to me.)

Late one evening, I stumbled into the spare bedroom and saw the light blinking on the answering machine. One message. I stabbed at the play button. At first, nothing. Then someone cleared his throat and muttered, "Man, don't you get it? God don't answer either." *Click.* No name. No number. Only silence.

I never discovered the caller's identity, but I do know one thing: He felt like God had deserted him. In the language of the Hebrew Scriptures, he felt as if God had "hidden his face"—as if God's face no longer shined on him. He felt as if the blessing of God was not for him.

Haven't you felt that way? I have. Before I pass through the pearly gates, I'll probably feel that way again. But here's the good news: God's steadfast love for his children was settled once and for all in Jesus Christ. Because of the one who embodied the benediction of God, God's face never stops shining on his children—even when his children feel that they are in the dark. In the words of the apostle Paul, "God ... gives us the light of the knowledge of God's glory in the face of Jesus Christ" (2 Cor 4:6).

That's why, on the evening of the Ascension, the disciples found themselves whooping it up in the temple courts instead of moping around the Mount of Olives. They knew that God's face was shining upon them, even when Jesus was no longer beside them.

Of course the shining face of God is no guarantee that our lives will be any easier. According to tradition, every apostle except John died a martyr because of the message of Jesus. What the shining face of God *does* guarantee is that nothing in all of creation can remove God's favor from the lives of his children.

What does that mean in your day-by-day life? It means that your children may rebel against you and your sewer lines may rupture beneath you. Your house may collapse around you, and your spirit may cry out within you. And yet, God's face will never stop shining upon you. You can't earn his shining face, and you can't exploit it. You can only embrace it by receiving the one whose face still shines "like the sun at full force" (Rv 1:16).

——A Meditation——

The shining face of God—
   the face that Moses could not see
   the face that sent prophets to their knees
   the face that speaks from eternity
     that face was present in this man from Galilee.
Oh shining face of God,
   please shine on me.

In the beginning was the Word, and the Word was with God, and the Word was God. He was in the beginning with God.... And the Word became flesh and lived among us, and we have seen his glory, the glory as of a father's only son, full of grace and truth.... No one has ever seen God. It is God the only Son, who is close to the Father's heart, who has made him known.

John 1:1-2, 14, 18, NRSV

After Jesus had spoken these words, he looked up to heaven and said, "Father, the hour has come; glorify your Son so that the Son may glorify you.... I glorified you on earth by finishing the work that you gave me to do. So now, Father, glorify me in your own presence with the glory that I had in your presence before the world existed.... I ask not only on behalf of these, but also on behalf of those who will believe in me through their word, that they may all be one. As you, Father, are in me and I am in you, may they also be in us, so that the world may believe that you have sent me. The glory that you have given me I have given them, so that they may be one, as we are one."

John 17:1, 4-5, 20-22, NRSV

The Glory of Prayer

In the beginning, there was nothing. Nothing at all. Nothing but God. God as Father, God as Son, God as Spirit. But only God. God and prayer.

Before the world came into being, the Father, Son, and Spirit lived in infinite, intimate fellowship with one another (see Jn 17:3, 24). What is prayer if not intimate fellowship with God? And what is the glory of God if not the splendor of this intimate fellowship?[1]

A word arose within this intimate fellowship and spawned a single pinpoint of infinite density. Suns and spheres appeared, swirling, twirling in an eternal dance. Peaks and plains exploded through seething oceans. On one tiny patch of earth, the hopes and dreams of the cosmos converged around a man, a woman, and a pair of trees. The fellowship of the woman and the man was a living reflection of the glorious fellowship of God (see Gn 1:26–27). And it was very good.

Then something unexplainable pierced the glory of God's good creation. Suddenly, all that had been so good became twisted into sin and sorrow and darkness and death. The specter of human selfishness engulfed the cosmos until only the dimmest reflections of glory remained.

In time, somewhere in the midst of that darkness a glimmer of glory arose again: "The true light—the light that enlightens everyone—was coming into the world" (Jn 1:9).

This time, it was not merely a reflection of God's glory that pierced the formless void. This time, the living God personally pierced the sinews of time and space.

Only a band of scruffy shepherds heard the first prayer of praise recorded after the arrival of God's glory: "Glory to God in the highest! And, on earth, peace to those with whom he is pleased!" (Lk 2:14).

Glory—the dazzling splendor of God's presence, veiled in human flesh. Glory—not on the wings of angels but in the virgin womb of a teenaged peasant. Glory—not on a cushion beside the crackling logs of a fireplace but in a feed-trough amid the steaming dung of sheep and goats.

The apostle John defined the glory of Jesus Christ with this phrase—it was "the glory of a Father's one and only son" (Jn 1:14). The glory of Jesus Christ was not his dazzling beauty and splendor— his glory was his fellowship with his Father.

How did Jesus sustain this glorious fellowship? "In the morning, while it was still dark, he would get up, go to a deserted place, and pray" (Mk 1:35). Even in the dark shadow of the cross, he prayed, "Abba, glorify your name" (Jn 12:27–28).

Through the prayers Jesus prayed, we are able to glimpse the inner life of God. We see ...

... a God who delights in doing the unexpected.

... a God who shatters our assumptions about his works and his ways.

... a God who desires to create a community that reflects his glory.

... a God who longs so deeply for a new future for us that he was willing to suffer and die to create it.

And that's not all. Just as importantly, the prayers Jesus prayed reveal that at the center of God's being, there is a glorious fellowship of prayer. God the Son brings his requests to God the Father; God the

Father praises his beloved Son; the Son prays that the Father will send the Spirit; the Spirit prays to the Father "with sighs that are beyond words"—and on and on the cycle moves, from eternity past to eternity future.[2]

That means that, when we pray, we are not merely sending a few sentences to the ruler of the universe—though that would be amazing enough by itself. Through prayer, we become "partakers in the divine nature" (2 Pt 1:4). We experience the infinite, inner fellowship of God. We receive a foretaste of the glorious future that God has planned for us.

Karl Barth once commented, "To clasp hands in prayer is the beginning of an uprising against the disorder of the world."[3] I think he was right. When I clasp my hands in prayer, I participate in the inner life of the One who longs to see his creation perfectly reflect his own glory, and who was willing to sacrifice himself to see his longing fulfilled.

——STUDY GUIDES——

by Linda R. McGinn

Each of these brief study guides is designed to help you reflect on the biblical truths revealed in this book and to enable you to explore portions of Scripture related to the ideas presented. The first section of each guide, "Consider Again," excerpts portions of the chapter and offers questions for personal or group study. The second section, "Reflections," enables you to look deeper into the meaning of several related biblical texts and apply their truth to your life.

The God Who Prays

Consider Again:

1. "No other religion in history includes a Supreme Being that prays—let alone a God who 'lives to intercede' for his people."

   A. What do you learn about the God of the Bible when you consider that he prays?

   B. What is intercession? How does it affect you to realize that God prays for his people?

2. "Most contemporary Christians have never even heard the prayers that Jesus learned and loved. In some sense, that limits our understanding of the Father who listened so intently to the prayers of his Son."

   A. What can reading the prayers that permeated the world in which Jesus lived teach us about his relationship with his heavenly Father?

   B. How do you think learning these prayers might influence the way you pray?

3. "For contemporary Christians prayer tends to be a *function*— an instrument to receive something from God. For the ancient Jews, prayer was a *lifestyle.*"

   A. What do you think it means for prayer to be a function?

   B. How would you describe a life in which prayer is a lifestyle rather than a function?

   C. Is prayer in your life a function or a lifestyle? Explain.

4. "The ancient Jews did not pray merely because they had needs that God could fulfill—they prayed because they lived every part of their lives as people who were united with God through an unbreakable covenant. Prayer was not merely a means to receive something *from* God, it was also a persistent expression of their life *in* God. Their very word for prayer, *tefilah,* had nothing to do with receiving anything from God. *Tefilah* means 'to discern what is in oneself.'"

    A. When defining prayer, what do you think it means "to discern what is in oneself"?

    B. Has prayer enabled you to discern what is in yourself? Illustrate.

    C. Will this definition affect your prayers in the future? Why or why not?

Reflections:

1. Read Psalm 139:1-6, 23-24

    A. What do you learn about God in verses 1-6 that qualifies him to reveal the inner thoughts of our hearts to us?

    B. How do verses 23-24 demonstrate the meaning of the Jewish word for prayer, *tefilah?*

2. Read John 17:11-26.

    A. How do verses 11-26 demonstrate Jesus' intercession?

    B. Do you believe Jesus prayed this prayer for you according to verse 20? Why or why not?

    C. How does the fact Jesus continues to pray for his people affect your life?

Chapter One
God's Unexpected Answer

Consider Again:

1. "Who would have believed that a girl with one foot still in puberty would soon have her other foot in motherhood— without placing either foot in a man's bed? Insanity? Yes. *Holy* insanity."

    A. Describe in your own words what the author means by "holy insanity."

    B. How do you think the presence and words of Simeon and Anna demonstrate "holy insanity"?

    C. Why do you think Mary's baby illustrates the "holy insanity" of God?

    D. Think of an incident in your life in which God revealed himself to you through "holy insanity."

2. "For centuries, the Jews' prayers for the Messiah had revolved around royal rulers and revolutions. In the midst of these misunderstandings, Simeon spoke a new prayer of expectation—a prayer that revolved around the revelation of God in the least likely place, in the tender flesh of a peasant's baby."

    A. Why was the baby, Jesus, the least likely place to find God?

    B. Describe a time when you found God in a least likely place.

Reflections:

1. Read Isaiah 55:8-9.

    A. What does verse 8 tell you about God's thoughts and ways?

    B. How do these verses confirm the reality of God's "holy insanity"?

    C. How were God's thoughts and ways "higher," according to verse 9, when he sent Jesus into the world as a baby?

2. Read John 1:1,14,18.

    A. "The Word" in verse 1 refers to Jesus Christ. What do you learn about Jesus from this verse?

    B. How does verse 14 describe the "holy insanity" of God?

    C. If no one has seen God, according to verse 18, who is "God the One and Only" and how has he made the Father God known?

    D. How did Jesus' coming as a baby to earth make the Father known? Has he made the Father known to you? Explain.

Chapter Two
The God Who Risks

Consider Again:

1. "The root of the Hebrew word for 'blessed,' *barukh*, means 'to bow.' The noun form means 'knee,' as in 'bow the knee.'"

    A. Define "blessed."

    B. How does God's incarnation in Jesus Christ demonstrate the meaning of *blessed*?

2. "If I truly bless someone, I do not merely wish him well; I submit to him. I give myself to him. I become vulnerable."

A. What does it mean to you that God desires to give himself to you?

B. How does it affect your understanding of God to realize he is willing to become vulnerable?

C. How does this knowledge of God affect your ability to become vulnerable for the sake of others?

3. "A *blessing* is a conscious choice to open myself to the possibility of pain and rejection. I can do a favor for someone and risk nothing. Not so when I bless someone."

A. Explain in your own words the difference between a blessing and a favor.

B. Do fears of rejection and pain cause you to hesitate to bless someone? Explain.

C. Why did God choose to become vulnerable?

4. "Blessedness is not about receiving things; it is about receiving God."

A. What do you think it means to receive God rather than things?

B. How did the incarnation of God in Jesus Christ allow you to receive God?

Reflections:

1. Read Deuteronomy 6:4-9.

A. What do you learn about God's will for his people in verses 4-5?

B. According to verses 6-9, how were God's people called to demonstrate their love?

C. How did prayer enable the Jewish people to follow God's directions in these verses?

D. Describe your prayer life. Does it enhance your ability to fulfill these verses? Why or why not?

2. Read Philippians 2:5-11.

    A. According to verse 5, how should your attitude be shaped throughout your life?

    B. Explain how verses 6-8 demonstrate the blessedness of God.

    C. In verses 9-11, what do you learn of the Father God's response to Jesus' vulnerability?

    D. What can you learn from Jesus' example about living your life? Explain.

Chapter Three
The Source of Joy

Consider Again:

1. "A dark, hungry void gnaws at every human being's innermost self."

    A. How would you describe the "dark, hungry void"?

    B. How is this reflected in a person's life?

2. "To embrace the implications of the [Jewish] wedding blessings is to admit that joy and pleasure are holy."

    A. What does it mean to admit that "joy and pleasure are holy"?

    B. Explain how a person seeks the infinite pleasure of God's presence.

    C. Describe moments in your life when you discovered the pleasure of God's presence through the ordinary pleasures of life.

3. "Our culture has attempted to replace authentic pleasure and joy with consumerism."

    A. List ways in which people in our culture attempt to replace pleasure and joy with consumerism.

    B. Describe a time when you turned to consumerism for pleasure.

4. "[Jesus'] earthly ministry began at an event permeated with implications of pleasure. His first miracle was to transform the plain water of a cultural ritual into an exquisite drink of exhilaration and joy."

    A. How did Jesus' first miracle, performed at the wedding at Cana, demonstrate the presence of God's pleasure in the midst of the world's counterfeit pleasures?

    B. Describe other methods God uses to demonstrate his pleasure in the midst of earthly counterfeit pleasures.

5. "How can we learn to live the *sheva b'rakhot?*... The first step is abandonment to the desire to unite my life with Jesus Christ."

    A. What were the *sheva b'rakhot?*

    B. What does "abandonment" mean? What does it *not* mean?

    C. How can your life reflect a life of abandonment to God?

Reflections:

1. Read Ephesians 1:9-10.

    A. What is God's good pleasure as described in these verses?

    B. How can you find pleasure in God through his Son, Jesus Christ?

2. Read 2 Timothy 3:4-5.

    A. Describe the behavior of those who seek pleasure without seeking God.

    B. Do you see these behaviors in our consumerist society? Illustrate.

    C. Do you see these behaviors in your own life? Why or why not?

3. Read Psalm 84:10-12.

    A. How does Psalm 84:10 illustrate a person whose heart desires the pleasure of God's presence?

    B. What is God's response to someone who seeks his pleasure?

    C. Write a prayer to God expressing your desire to experience his love and pleasure as never before.

Chapter Four
God's Unwelcome Answer

Consider Again:

1. "The Nazarenes had prayed, 'Dwell in Zion!' and God had answered their prayer. In the words of the apostle John, 'The Word became flesh and dwelt among them' (Jn 1:14). But God pitched his tent on his own terms and in his own way. The Nazarenes simply couldn't stomach the thought that God might drive his tent-stakes beyond the Jewish people."

    A. What difficult answer did the citizens of Nazareth receive from God when they prayed, "Dwell in Zion"?

    B. Why was it difficult?

    C. In what ways do contemporary Christians find God's answer to this prayer difficult?

2. "Will we recognize and accept the unwelcome answers to our prayers, even though these answers may cost us deeply? Or will we, like the Jews in Nazareth, clench so tightly to our misguid-

ed assumptions that we can't see the answer to our prayers even when the answer is standing in front of us?"

    A. Describe the two paths we can take in response to prayer.

    B. Which path characterizes your prayer life? Explain.

3. "God ... defied their expectations because he longed to give them something greater than their expectations.... That's how God answers our prayers. Whenever his answer *defies* our expectations it also *surpasses* our expectations."

    A. How would you describe your usual expectations when you pray?

    B. Describe a time when God gave you something greater than your expectations in response to prayer.

4. "In our attempt to avoid insincere prayers, Christians frequently go to the other extreme—praying prayers that are sincere but petty."

    A. What would you consider "petty prayers"? Give an example.

    B. Describe the type of prayers you could pray instead of these petty ones.

Reflections:

1. Read John 11:3, 21-26, 40-44.

    A. What did the sisters Martha and Mary request from Jesus in verse 3?

    B. According to verse 21, did they receive a difficult answer from him?

    C. How was God's answer greater than their expectations?

2. Read Matthew 7:7-11.

    A. According to verses 7-8, what can you expect from God when you pray?

      B. How do verses 9-11 characterize God's answers to prayer?

3. Read Matthew 17:19-21.

      A. What were the disciples requesting from God in prayer?

      B. How was their prayer answered? Why was it answered in this way?

      C. What is Jesus' promise in answer to prayer? How could this truth cause you to move from petty, human-sized prayers to mighty, God-sized prayers? (For further reflection, read Mathew 19:26, Mark 10:27, Luke 1:37 and 18:27.)

Chapter Five
Looking for the Kingdom

Consider again:

1. "We were simply a band of pilgrims who shared a common prayer because we had undertaken a common journey toward the kingdom of God. In that moment, nearly a decade ago, I recognized that the Lord's Prayer is not simply a prayer. It is a *signpost*—a signpost that binds the people of God together and keeps them pointed toward God's kingdom."

      A. What is the "common journey" spoken of here?

      B. Explain how the Lord's Prayer is a "signpost" that keeps the people of God pointed in the same direction.

      C. How could the Lord's Prayer become a signpost in your life?

2. "Only in the Lord's Prayer did Jesus call his Father '*our* Father.' His original words were probably even more overwhelming. More than likely, Jesus called his Father '*Abba*'—an Aramaic appellation that combined tender intimacy with profound

respect. Every child in Judea had addressed his or her father as Abba, but no one had ever addressed God in this way."

    A. What does it mean that Jesus combined "tender intimacy with profound respect" when praying to God?

    B. How does this fact affect your prayer life?

3. "To pray the Lord's Prayer is to ask Abba to be fully present here and now, in us. When Abba is present in our lives, we become the realm in which God is hallowing his name. Then, nothing, absolutely nothing, can remain the same."

    A. Define the word "hallowed" in relationship to God's name.

    B. What does it mean to become "the realm in which God is hallowing his name"?

    C. Explain why nothing can remain the same when we begin to realize that God is fully present here and now, in us. How will this truth affect your life today?

Reflections:

1. Read Psalm 84:5.

    A. What is the source of blessing in this verse?

    B. What actions are we encouraged to take concerning our pilgrimage with God?

2. Read John 14:15-21.

    A. How does Abba—"the Father"—dwell in us, according to verses 15-18?

    B. What is Jesus' promise for you in verse 21?

186 / Prayers Jesus Prayed

Chapter Six
The God Who Hears

Consider Again:

1. "He doesn't want me to thank him because he always gives me what I want—after all, he *doesn't* always give me what I want. He wants me to thank him because he has taken the time to listen to me. He wants to hear my prayers of gratitude not because of *what he gives* but because of *who he is*."

    A. How do we know that God listens to us when we pray?

    B. List the character qualities of God for which you are thankful.

2. "At the secret heart of all our prayers, what we really want is not an answer but an assurance—an assurance that our Abba is listening. The prayer of Jesus in the garden is our assurance that he is."

    A. What "need" do we have according to this statement?

    B. How did the prayer of Jesus at Lazarus' tomb meet this need?

    C. How will this fact affect your future prayers?

Reflections:

1. Read Psalm 7:17, 100:5, 107:1, and Psalm 136.

    A. For what character qualities can we thank God, according to Psalms 7:17, 100:5, and 107:1?

    B. Read Psalm 136 aloud as a prayer of thanks to the Lord.

    C. Psalm 136 retells the history of Israel, listing the times that God listened to his people's prayers. The psalmist punctuated each sentence with the refrain, "His steadfast love never ends." Use this format to write your own prayer of thanksgiving, listing incidents where God has worked in your life. Read it aloud in prayer.

2. Read 2 Kings 20:5 and Hebrews 4:14-16.

   A. What do you learn from 2 Kings 20:5 about God's regard for your tears of pain and sorrow?

   B. What do you learn from Hebrews 4:14-16 about Jesus and his response to the difficulties in your life?

3. Read Isaiah 59:1.

   A. What do you learn from this verse about God's ability to hear your prayers?

   B. How does the fact that God hears your prayers affect the way that you respond to the problems in your life?

Chapter Seven
The God Who Remembers

Consider Again:

1. "What made the Passover special was not the meal—it was the memory. It was as if, once each year, God sat down at the table with his people, opened a tattered scrapbook, and recounted the story of his relationship with them."

   A. What was God's purpose in asking his people to remember?

   B. What did God want his people to remember?

2. "It was as if God was telling his disciples, 'Not only did I remember my promise to your ancestors—I made a new promise and signed it in my own blood. Not only did I remember to send the Messiah—I *became* the Messiah. Not only did I remember the holy city, I am turning *you* into a holy city. I have remembered you. Now, you remember me.'"

188 / *Prayers Jesus Prayed*

    A. What was the new promise God made through Jesus? How did he sign it in his own blood?

    B. Explain what it means that God is turning us into a holy city.

3. "Why do so many people keep returning to the Lord's Table week after week? In order to commemorate and remember the God who has chosen never to forget us. 'I will not forget you,' he promised his people. 'Look, I have inscribed you on the palms of my hands' (Is 49:16)."

    A. What memory does Holy Communion commemorate?

    B. Explain what God meant when he said he had inscribed his people on the palms of his hands.

Reflections:

1. Read Exodus 3:14-15.

    A. Why did God want to be remembered by the phrase "I AM WHO I AM"?

    B. What were God's people instructed through Moses to do in these verses? How can you fulfill this desire of God?

2. Read Psalm 77:11-12.

    A. According to these verses, what are we to remember and consider?

    B. How will reading this chapter affect your attitude toward the Lord's Supper in your church?

Chapter Eight
One God, One People

Consider Again:

1. "Jesus' prayer for unity as he made his way across the Kidron

Valley is ... a thin place. Through this prayer, we gain a tiny, glimmering hint of the inner splendor of God. And what we see at the center of God's being is not blinding light or raw power but a glorious relationship."

    A. What does Timothy mean by a "thin place"?

    B. What do you learn about this "glorious relationship" from the prayer for unity?

2. "If I take this prayer for unity seriously, I must give up the arrogant illusion that my salvation, my spiritual life, and my sins are personal matters.... To follow Jesus, I need the fellowship of other believers. So do you, and so has every saint in the history of the church."

    A. Why is it an "arrogant illusion" to believe we can live the Christian life alone?

    B. What does the fellowship of fellow believers offer the individual Christian?

3. "The world will be won not through the wisdom of our words but through the witness of our oneness."

    A. What is the meaning of the phrase, "the world will be won"?

    B. Explain "the witness of our oneness."

    C. How can you help to make this witness possible?

Reflections:

1. Read Philippians 2:1-2.

    A. What benefits are listed in verse 1 that Christians can experience?

    B. How, in verse 2, does Paul ask believers to respond to these benefits? How can this become a witness to the world?

2. Read Colossians 2:1-3.

   A. What was the purpose of Paul's struggle, recorded in verse 2?

   B. What is the benefit of the unity described in verses 2-3?

   C. How can unity with the church benefit you in your spiritual journey? Offer examples.

3. Read Ephesians 4:1-4, 11-13.

   A. What directions are given in verses 1-4 for helping you to discover unity in the body of Christ?

   B. What is the benefit of diversity in the body of Christ?

   C. What role has God given you in his body? How can your role contribute to God's plan and purpose?

Chapter Nine
Praying in the Darkness

Consider Again:

1. "Why didn't the crucified Christ curse anyone? Because on the cross, he *became* the curse. He did not curse because he *was* the curse.... Jesus did not merely bear the pain of God's punishment for sin, he became the pain, the shame, the curse of humanity's sin."

   A. Why was it necessary for Jesus to do this?

   B. How does the fact Jesus became the curse affect your life?

2. "The central image of the Christian faith is ... a cross—not a set of scales."

   A. What does "a set of scales" represent in this statement?

   B. Give an illustration of the difference between the cross and a set of scales.

   C. Which characterizes your attitude toward others' failures—the cross or a set of scales? Explain.

3. "God the Father has cursed him, forsaken him, and caused him to become the essence of sin, but Jesus never gives up on his Father's love. He does not merely trust his Father; he trusts his Father with ... '*ruthless trust.*'"

    A. Define "ruthless trust."

    B. Do you trust God with ruthless trust? Why or why not?

Reflections:

1. Read Deuteronomy 11:1, 13-14, 22, 26-28.

    A. What were the Jewish people commanded to do?

    B. What was to be the result of their disobedience?

2. Read Deuteronomy 2:22-23.

    A. Who was under God's curse?

    B. If Jesus embodied the sin of all humanity, what effect should his crucifixion have on your life?

3. Read Galatians 3:10-13.

    A. Why is freedom from the curse of God dependent on a relationship rather than a keeping of rules, according to verse 10?

    B. According to verses 11-12, why is faith so important?

    C. According to verses 13-14, what promise did Jesus secure for believers through his crucifixion?

4. Read Luke 6:27-28, Romans 12:14.

    A. According to Luke's Gospel, what does Jesus teach us about the way we are to treat others since he has removed the curse of sin in our lives?

    B. Who does Paul tell us to bless, and how does Jesus model this for us?

5. Read Revelation 22:3-5.

    A. Who is the Lamb referred to in verse 3?

    B. What is the promise of this verse for all believers in Jesus Christ?

Chapter Ten
May the Lord Make His Face to Shine Upon You

Consider Again:

1. "It was one thing to worship Jesus while his feet were on the ground. But to worship him after he was gone was to confess that somehow he was still present among them."

    A. How was Jesus still present among the disciples after he ascended into the heavens?

    B. How does our worship confess our belief that Jesus is alive and present among us?

2. "By the time Jesus blessed his disciples on the Mount of Olives, the people of Israel had heard the benediction for fifteen centuries. But only Jesus *became* the benediction."

    A. How did Jesus become "the benediction of God"?

    B. How is Jesus the benediction of God in your life?

3. "Because of the one who embodied the benediction of God, God's face never stops shining on his children—even when his children feel that they are in the dark."

    A. What assurance do we have that God's light is always shining on his people?

    B. How can you be assured of God's light even when you feel nothing but darkness?

    C. Describe a time when God confirmed the light of his presence during a dark time in your life.

Reflections:

1. Read Luke 24:36-39, 45-49.

    A. What did Jesus cite as proof of resurrection in verses 36-39?

    B. According to verses 45-49, what was Jesus' blessing upon his followers?

C. How does this blessing apply to you today?

2. Read Isaiah 60:1-3, 19-20.

    A. What is God's promise to the Jewish people in verses 1-3?

    B. How does that promise extend to us today in Jesus Christ?

    C. What hope do verses 19-20 offer you today?

Afterword
The Glory of Prayer

Consider Again:

1. "The glory of Jesus Christ was not his dazzling beauty and splendor—his glory was his fellowship with his Father. How did Jesus sustain this glorious relationship? 'In the morning, while it was still dark, he would get up, go to a deserted place, and pray' (Mk 1:35)."

    A. What is the source of glory?

    B. What can be learned from Jesus' example, as recorded in Mark 1:35?

    C. How can you experience God's glory?

2. "Through prayer, we become 'partakers in the divine nature' (2 Pt 1:4). We experience the infinite inner fellowship of God. We receive a foretaste of the glorious future that God has planned for us."

    A. What does it mean to be "partakers in the divine nature"?

    B. In what ways will eternity be an extension of our present life with God on earth?

    C. Is your life with God on earth preparing you for heaven? Why or why not?

Reflections:

1. Read Hebrews 1:3.

    A. How does God speak to us, according to verses 1-2?

    B. What do you learn about Jesus from verses 3-4?

    C. What do you learn about God's glory from these verses?

2. Read 2 Corinthians 3:18.

    A. What does it mean to have "unveiled faces"?

    B. What is God doing in your life to help you to reflect "the glory of the Lord"?

    C. Give one example of this personal transformation.

3. Read Romans 8:17.

    A. What is the result of sharing in Jesus' suffering?

    B. If God's glory is a result of a relationship with God, what assurance do you have of God's presence during difficult times?

ONE
God's Unexpected Answer

1. Leviticus 1:14–17; 5:7–10. See Walter C. Kaiser, Jr., "Leviticus," in *New Interpreter's Bible* vol. 1 (Nashville, Tenn.: Abingdon, 1994), 1013–14.

2. A few scholars believe that Jesus was not redeemed and therefore remained the special property of God. See Bo Reicke, "Jesus, Simeon, and Anna," in *Saved by Hope*, ed. J.I. Cook (Grand Rapids, Mich.: Eerdmans, 1978), 100, and Charles H. Talbert, *Reading Luke* (New York: Crossroad, 1992), 36–38. While this hypothesis makes sense theologically, it does not fit the biblical text. Choosing not to redeem a firstborn child was not "customary according to the Law" (Lk 2:27; cf. Ex 13:13; Nm 18:15).

3. Exodus 13:2; Numbers 18:15–16.

4. This reconstruction of the liturgy for the redemption of firstborn sons is adapted from A.Z. Idelsohn, *Jewish Liturgy and Its Development* (New York: Schocken, 1962), 167–68, and A. Millgram, *Jewish Worship* (Philadelphia: Jewish Publication Society, 1971), 323–24.

5. Numbers 6:23–25.

6. Jews in the first half of the first century may have prayed the Amidah daily. However, the earliest reference of this practice stems from A.D. 80 (see the reference to Rabban Gamaliel II in *m. Berakhoth* 4:3). (References to *The Mishnah* [Philadelphia: Jewish

Publication Society] are indicated by "m." followed by the tractate title, then section and verse numbers.)

7. Not all recensions of the Amidah conclude with this plea. However, even if this prayer of expectation postdates the birth of Jesus, it still expresses the essential messianic expectations of first-century Judaism.

8. Moses Ben-Maimonides, *Mishneh Torah, Sefer Shoftim, Hilchot Melachim U'Milchamoteihem,* 11. Although Moses Ben-Maimonides was a medieval rabbi, the lines quoted here probably reflect earlier Jewish messianic expectations. I have excluded some lines written by Ben-Maimonides, which seem to be responses to the rise of Christianity and to the destruction of the Jewish temple in A.D.70.

9. Reconstructed from the Dead Sea Scroll fragment 1Q34:5:1.

10. "The redemption of Jerusalem" echoes the Messianic prophecy in Isaiah 52:7–10.

11. Frederick Buechner, *The Hungering Dark* (New York: HarperSanFrancisco, 1985), 14.

TWO
The God Who Risks

1. *Hallel* means "praise." These songs of praise comprise Psalms 113—18 in the English Bible.

2. The *tallith* is a special shawl, worn during the morning prayer services. *Tefillin* are tiny boxes (also known as *phylacteries*) which Jewish males strapped to their hands and to their foreheads. In literal obedience to Exodus 13:9, 16, the boxes contained passages of Scripture.

3. Today, a Jewish male becomes a "son of the commandments" (bar mitzvah) when he reaches thirteen—a practice that was not widespread until the fifteenth century A.D. When a Jewish male turned twelve in the first century A.D., he "would be in Jewish terms beginning to make the transition into adult responsibility under the law" (J. Nolland, *Luke 1–9:20* in *Word Biblical Commentary* vol. 35a [Dallas: Word, 1989], 129). "At the age of twelve the instruction of boys became more intensive in preparation of the recognition of adulthood" (D.L. Bock, *Luke* [Grand Rapids: Zondervan, 1996], 99).

4. Cf. Deuteronomy 30:11–14. Prophets and rabbis frequently referred to the Law of Moses as a "yoke" (cf., e.g., Jer 2:20; 5:5; see also Acts 15:10; Gal 5:1). When Jesus said that his "yoke was easy" (Mt 11:29–30), he used a popular depiction of the Torah to identify himself as the fulfillment of the Law.

5. Cf. A. Millgram, *Jewish Worship* (Philadelphia: Jewish Publication Society, 1971), 96–101. The Shema is the central expression of the Jewish faith. The Hebrew word *Shema* means "hear" or "obey." It is drawn from the opening phrase of Deuteronomy 6:4. In the first century, the recitation of the Shema probably consisted of a blessing, three Scripture passages, and another blessing. The Scriptures were Deuteronomy 6:4–9, Deuteronomy 11:13–21, and Numbers 15:37–41. For the sake of brevity, I have condensed the Scripture passages.

6. The word *blessed* is the English translation of the Hebrew word *barukh.*

7. See http://www.jewfaq.org/prayer.htm.

8. Notice the connection between blessedness and God's name in Exodus 20:24; Numbers 6:27; Psalm 63:4, et al.

9. Joni Eareckson Tada and Steve Estes, *When God Weeps: Why Our*

Sufferings Matter to the Almighty (Grand Rapids: Zondervan, 1997), 45.

10. Philip Yancey, *The Jesus I Never Knew* (Grand Rapids: Zondervan, 1995), 36.

11. Thomas Cahill, *Desire of the Everlasting Hills* (New York: Doubleday, 1999), 89.

12. Brennan Manning, *The Ragamuffin Gospel* rev. ed. (Sisters, Ore.: Multnomah, 2000), 167.

13. Some phrases in this prayer were drawn from Ken Taylor, *Praying the Passion: Daily Readings and Prayers for Lent* (Nashville, Tenn.: Abingdon, 2000), 21.

THREE
The Source of Joy

1. Luke 3:14.

2. One "stadium" equaled the distance of a race in a Roman stadium, roughly one-fifth of a kilometer. Biblical scholars are uncertain of the exact location of Cana. The location described here— fifteen kilometers north of Nazareth, approximately halfway between the Sea of Galilee and the Mediterranean Sea—is the most probable suggestion.

3. Cf. 3 Maccabees 4:6. The *kallah* was the bride; the *chatan* was the groom. Ten silver coins seem to have constituted the minimum dowry that the *ketubah* (marriage contract) guaranteed the bride. This dowry remained hers, even if the marriage was dissolved (cf. Craig S. Keener's comments in *The IVP Bible Background Commentary: New Testament* [Downers Grove, Ill.: InterVarsity, 1993], 232). The coins were drachmae or denarii. Each coin was

worth approximately one day's wages. According to some reconstructions, first-century women wore the ten coins in a crown. The authenticity of this tradition is uncertain, but it is certainly plausible. Luke 15:8 may refer to this custom.

4. Cf. Isaiah 61:10; 3 Maccabees 4:8. This declaration is found in the Elephantine papyri. In contemporary Judaism, the betrothal (*erusin*) and the wedding (*nissu'im*) occur in the same ceremony. In the first century, the betrothal usually took place several months before the wedding, although it could occur immediately before the wedding (cf. Tb 7:21-8:1).

5. Nathanael was from Cana (Jn 21:2) and seems to have been Jesus' only connection to Cana. ("Simon the Cananaean" was not from Cana; "Cananaean" is Aramaic for "Zealot.") Therefore, in the context of John 1:43-2:11, it is possible that the wedding was for a relative or close friend of Nathanael and that Jesus, his mother Mary, and the other disciples attended the feast as Nathanael's guests. In the other Gospels, Nathanael is called "Bartholomew" (literally, "Bar-Tolmai"), which means "Tolmai's son."

6. Luke 1:33.

7. It is difficult to reconstruct the marriage blessings that would have been used around A.D. 30. After the destruction of the Jewish temple in A.D. 70, additional lines were inserted into the blessings, asking God to restore joy and gladness to Jerusalem. I have adapted this reconstruction from several rabbinic tractates and from A. Millgram, *Jewish Worship* (Philadelphia: Jewish Publication Society, 1971), 328-29; A.Z. Idelsohn, *Jewish Liturgy and Its Development* (New York: Schocken, 1960), 169-70; R. Posner, et al., *Jewish Liturgy* (Jerusalem: Keter, 1975), 238; and http://www.ahavat-israel.com/torat/.

8. Blaise Pascal, *Penseés*, 425.

9. Augustine of Hippo, *Confessions,* 1:1.

10. In terms of frequency, the depiction of God as Israel's lover (Is 54:1-7; 62:4-5; Jer 2:2; 2:29-32; 3:20; 31:32; Ez 16:1-63; 23: 1-49; Hos 2:1-3:5) is second only to the image of God as the sovereign king (Is 6:5; 33:17-22; 41:21; 43:15; 44:6; Jer 10:6-10; 46:18; 48:15; 51:57; Ez 20:33; Dan 4:37; Zep 3:15; 14:9-19; Mal 1:14).

11. Leonard I. Sweet, *SoulTsunami: Sink or Swim in New Millennium Culture* (Grand Rapids: Zondervan, 1999), 423. For the ancient Hebrews' view of sexual pleasure, see, e.g., Song of Solomon 1, 4-7; Tobit 8:4-9.

12. Manning, *The Ragamuffin Gospel* rev. ed., 88-89.

13. Carol Memmott, "Buy into Hilarious 'Shopaholic' Binge," review of Sophie Kinsella, *Confessions of a Shopaholic,* in *USA Today,* 15 February 2001, sec. 4D.

14. Walter Burkhardt, *Still Proclaiming Your Wonders* (Mahwah, N.J.: Paulist, 1984), 168.

15. Quoted in Brennan Manning, *Ruthless Trust: The Ragamuffin's Path to God* (New York: Harper, 2000), 69.

16. In the writings of the apostle John, the first event at which Jesus Christ reveals his identity is a wedding. So is the last. The final event in the book of Revelation is the marriage of Jesus Christ to his people (cf. Rv 19–22).

17. Brennan Manning, *Lion and Lamb: The Relentless Tenderness of Jesus* (Grand Rapids: Chosen, 1986), 58, 90.

18. Some portions of this prayer are drawn from the benediction in Manning, *Lion and Lamb,* 124-25.

FOUR

God's Unwelcome Answer

1. The first-century form of these benedictions is uncertain. This rendering is one possible reconstruction of the first-century A.D. form of the benedictions that Jews also refer to as *Ha-Tefillah* (the Prayer). After the time of Christ, the Council of Yavneh (Jamnia) expanded the *Amidah*. Today, the *Amidah* is known as the *Shemoneh Esrei* or Eighteen Benedictions.

2. The *chazan* was the custodian of the synagogue, the caretaker of the scrolls, and in some cases, the teacher of Jewish children in the community. Luke 4:20 refers to the chazan as "the attendant."

3. See Luke 4:22.

4. Cf. Matthew 23:6; Luke 11:43.

5. The prayers in this chapter are drawn from several sources, including C.W. Dugmore, *The Influence of the Synagogue Upon the Divine Office* (Oxford: Oxford University, 1944), 115-24; Everett Ferguson, *Backgrounds of Early Christianity* 2nd ed. (Grand Rapids: Eerdmans, 1993), 539-46; Emil Schürer, *The History of the Jewish People in the Age of Jesus Christ*, ed. G. Vermes, et al. (Edinburgh: T&T Clark, 1979), 2:456-61.

6. Luke 4:18–19a. The reading is a paraphrase of Isaiah 61:1-2, with the words "and a day of vengeance" omitted and a phrase from Isaiah 58:6 added.

7. Christopher J.H. Wright, *Knowing Jesus Through the Old Testament*, as quoted in Philip Yancey, *The Bible Jesus Read* (Grand Rapids, Mich.: Zondervan, 1999), 185-86.

8. Rich Mullins, "Hold Me, Jesus," *A Liturgy, a Legacy, and a Ragamuffin Band* (Nashville, Tenn.: Reunion, 1993), audio.

9. C.S. Lewis, *The Weight of Glory and Other Addresses* (Grand Rapids, Mich.: Eerdmans, 1965), 1-2.

10. Eugene Peterson, *A Long Obedience in the Same Direction* (Downers Grove, Ill.: InterVarsity, 1980), 190.

11. C.S. Lewis, *The Lion, the Witch, and the Wardrobe* (New York: Macmillan, 1950), 75-76.

12. Frederick Buechner, *Wishful Thinking* rev. ed. (New York: HarperCollins, 1993), 87.

FIVE
Looking for the Kingdom

1. R.T. France, *The Gospel According to Matthew: An Introduction and Commentary* (Grand Rapids, Mich.: Eerdmans, 1985), 134; Robert Guelich, *The Sermon on the Mount* (Dallas: Word, 1982), 310.

2. Paraphrased from *The Union Prayerbook for Jewish Worship* rev. ed. (Cincinnati: CCAR, 1948), 342.

3. Guelich, 313; E. Moore, "Lead Us Not Into Temptation," *Expository Times* 102 (1991): 171-72.

4. Galilean Jews, who rarely sailed on large ships, referred to the Sea of Galilee as a "sea." It is, more precisely, a lake. Roman soldiers, for whom sailing the Mediterranean Sea was a way of life, scornfully called the Sea of Galilee "the pond."

5. The Gospels imply that when Jesus began performing miracles, the crowds around him grew rapidly (cf. Mt 4:23-25; Lk 5:12–15). When Jesus refused to do miracles at the people's request, the crowds diminished (Jn 6:25-34, 60-66).

6. During his Galilean ministry, Jesus seems to have stayed at Simon's home in Capernaum (Mt 4:13; Mk 1:21, 29-33; 2:1-3; 9:33)

7. I have used "congratulations" to translate the Greek term *makarios* in this text. Although "blessed" is the usual rendering of *makarios,* "congratulations" captures the word's meaning more accurately. *Makarios* is the Greek equivalent of the Hebrew root-word *ashr,* which means "contented," "cheerful," "gifted," "congratulated," even "happy-go-lucky." (The translators of the French New Testament were on the right track when they rendered Matthew's third beatitude, *"Heureux sont les débonnaires"* ["Cheerful are the debonair"].) The meaning that the English term "blessed" properly reflects is expressed through the Hebrew root-word *brkh* ("blessed," "bowed to") and its Greek equivalent *eulogetes* ("blessed," "thanked") (see, e.g., Lk 6:28). Although the meanings of *brkh, eulogetes,* and "blessed" overlap with *ashr, makarios,* and "congratulations," the two word groups are not synonymous. Cf. G. Bertram, "*makarios,*" in *Theologisches Worterbuch Neuen Testament* vol. 4, ed. G. Kittel (Stuttgart: Kohlhammer Verlag, 1964); H.W. Beyer, "*eulogetein,*" in *Theologisches Worterbuch Neuen Testament* vol. 2; Charles Talbert, *Reading Luke* (New York: Crossroad, 1992), 72.

8. The Sermon on the Mount (Mt 5-7) and the Sermon on the Plain (Lk 6:20–49) seem to be variations of a message that Jesus preached in several ways in several places (cf. discussions in Guelich, 35; Nolland, 283-87). This reconstruction includes portions of each sermon. Luke 6:20-27 and Matthew 6:14-15 are my own translations. Matthew 5:45 and 6:1, 5-8 are taken from *The Message.*

9. Portions of this paragraph allude to "A Peace of the Rock," *Preaching* (July-August 1995), 43-44.

10. Luke 17:20–21. The King James Version mistranslates Luke 17:21 as "the kingdom of God is *in* you." The Greek preposition

"*en*" means "in" only when followed by a singular noun or pronoun. In Luke 17:21, the Greek word translated "you" (*humon*) is plural. When followed by a plural noun or pronoun, "*en*" means "among," not "in."

11. The meaning of "the kingdom of God" and "the kingdom of heaven" shifts slightly between the Synoptic Gospels (Matthew, Mark, and Luke) and the rest of the New Testament. In the Synoptic Gospels, the kingdom is *God's presence in Jesus Christ.* In the rest of the New Testament (especially in Paul's epistles), the kingdom is *the realm of God's work on earth which will be revealed at the end of time.* Both realities are, however, rooted in the presence and the plan of God the Father.

12. R.T. France, 134; Guelich, 310.

13. Although English translations usually render the opening phrase of the Lord's Prayer "Our Father in heaven," the phrase is, literally, "our Father in *the heavens*" or "our Father in *the skies.*" In this context, "the heavens" seems to be a metaphor for the eternal realm—i.e., God is, in contrast to humanity, infinite and holy.

14. Peter van Breemen, *Called by Name* (Denville, N.J.: Dimension, 1976), 43; cf. Brennan Manning, *The Signature of Jesus* rev. ed. (Sisters, Oregon: Multnomah, 1996), 170.

15. Joachim Jeremias, *The Prayers of Jesus* (Naperville, Ill.: Allenson, 1967), 58–62. The Hebrew Scriptures refer to God as "father" fifteen times (Dt 32:6; Jer 3:4, 19; 31:9; 2 Sm 7:14; 1 Chr 17:13; 22:10; 28:6; Is 63:16; 64:8; Mal 1:6; 2:10; Ps 68:5; 89:26; 103:13).

16. Manning, *The Ragamuffin Gospel* rev. ed., 28, 55.

17. Cf., e.g., B. Nicholas, et al., "*patria potestas,*" in *The Oxford Classical Dictionary,* ed. Simon Hornblower and Anthony Spawforth (Oxford: Oxford University Press, 1996), 1122-123.

18. Quoted in Simon Tugwell, *The Beatitudes* (Springfield, Ill.: Templegate, 1980), 138.

19. Walter Wangerin, Jr., *Reliving the Passion* (Grand Rapids, Mich.: Zondervan, 1992), 66.

20. Frederick Buechner, *Listening to Your Life,* as quoted in William Willimon and Stanley Hauerwas, *Lord, Teach Us: The Lord's Prayer and the Christian Life* (Nashville, Tenn.: Abingdon, 1996), 9.

SIX
The God Who Hears

1. See *m. Kethub.* 4:4. Women were frequently hired to mourn the deceased person's death for thirty days after the burial. An upper middle-class family such as Lazarus' family would also have hired at least two flutists to play somber dirges during the time of mourning. Cf. Ben Witherington III, *Women in the Ministry of Jesus: A Study of Jesus' Attitude to Women and their Roles as Reflected in his Earthly Life* (Cambridge: Cambridge University, 1984), 74–75.

2. *m. Kethub.* 8.

3. Centuries from now, archaeologists will unearth this charred chunk of chocolate and dough and will write brilliant (albeit erroneous) articles about American culinary culture in the late twentieth century.

4. Quoted in Philip Yancey, *The Bible Jesus Read* (Grand Rapids, Mich.: Zondervan, 1999), 35.

5. Mark Buchanan, "Jesus Wept," in *Christianity Today,* 5 March 2001, 68.

SEVEN

The God Who Remembers

1. William Willimon and Stanley Hauerwas, *Lord, Teach Us: The Lord's Prayer and the Christian Life* (Nashville, Tenn.: Abingdon, 1996), 17, 21, 28.

2. This reconstruction of a first-century Passover liturgy is based on *m. Pesahim* 10:1–9; Deuteronomy 26:5–8; R. Alan Culpepper, "Luke," in *New Interpreter's Bible* vol. 7 (Nashville, Tenn.: Abingdon, 1995), 418–19; Joachim Jeremias, *The Eucharistic Words of Jesus* (Philadelphia: Fortress, 1966), 84–88; Ceil Rosen, *Christ in the Passover* (Chicago: Moody, 1978), 41–72; and Anthony J. Saldarini, *Jesus and Passover* (Ramsey, N.J.: Paulist, 1984), 32–50.

3. Saldarini, 69.

4. John 13:20.

5. The participants in the Exodus had to leave Egypt quickly. Roasted meat and unleavened bread could be prepared more quickly than boiled meat and leavened bread. Therefore roasted meat and unleavened bread became the symbols of their deliverance from Egypt. Because roasted meat tended to be tough, boiled meat was preferred in the ancient world.

6. For the sake of brevity, I have condensed this portion of the Passover Seder.

7. I have only translated selected portions from the first section of the Hallel (Psalms 113–14). In the actual Seder, they would have chanted the entire first part of the Hallel.

8. This was the second of four cups that the disciples drank during the Passover meal. After Jesus drank from the first cup, he said,

"From now on, I will not drink of the fruit of the vine until God's kingdom comes" (Lk 22:18). He repeated this vow when he served the third cup (Mt 26:29; Mk 14:25).

9. The Passover Seder (literally, "order") is the basic outline of the entire ceremony, encompassing all of the psalms, Scriptures, prayers, questions, answers, and liturgical activities that occur during the Passover service.

10. The perspective from which I have retold the Last Supper is that of John Mark. It isn't certain that Mark was present at the Last Supper, but it is certainly plausible. The disciples continued to meet in the upper room after the resurrection (Acts 1:13). And when Simon Peter was released from prison, he knew it was in the home of Mark's mother that the church would be meeting for prayer (Acts 12:11-12). Also, only the Gospel of Mark includes this obscure passage: "A certain young man, wearing nothing but a linen cloth, had followed Jesus [from the Upper Room]. They caught hold of him, but he left the linen cloth and ran off naked" (Mk 14:51-52). Perhaps John Mark surreptitiously followed Jesus and the disciples into the Garden of Gethsemane, and then fled. If so, it is probably to John Mark that we owe the record of Jesus' prayers in the garden—Peter, James, and John were, after all, asleep.

11. The "giving thanks" mentioned in Luke 22:19 and 1 Corinthians 11:24 would have included the Birkat Ha-Mazon.

12. Cf. Revelation 21, where the people of God—the bride of Christ—are identified as the holy city.

EIGHT
One God, One People

1. Unless otherwise indicated, I have used *The Message* to render John 16:29-18:1.
2. From Culpepper, 462.
3. Willimon and Hauerwas, 28, 29, 77, 108.
4. Quoted in James Bryan Smith, *Rich Mullins: An Arrow Pointing to Heaven* (Nashville, Tenn.: Broadman & Holman, 2000), 33.
5. Walter Burkhardt, *Tell the Next Generation* (Ramsey, N.J.: Paulist, 1982), 114.
6. Some phrases in this prayer are drawn from Taylor, 25.

NINE
Praying in the Darkness

1. The Romans viewed the sun's absence as one sign of the death of a divine ruler. The poet Virgil wrote concerning Caesar's death, "The sun shall give you signs. (Who would dare say that the sun might lie?).... After the Caesar sank from sight, he wrapped his countenance in darkened gloom, and a godless generation feared endless night" (Virgil, *Georgics,* in Loeb Classical Library [Cambridge: Harvard, 1978], 1:113).
2. According to Roman practice, the friends and family of the crucified person had to stand at a distance from the cross, to prevent rescue attempts. On extremely rare occasions, persons *were* rescued from crosses, after their friends overpowered, begged, or bribed the guards. The trauma of crucifixion was, however, so great that survival was rare. The Jewish historian Josephus rescued three friends from crosses. Only one of them survived. See

Josephus, *Vita*, sec. 420.

3. Despite the familiar image of a woven crown of thorns, it is more likely that the Roman soldiers uprooted a small thorn bush, twisted it quickly, and shoved it onto the head of Jesus. This understanding does not contradict the intent of the words translated "twisted" and "wove" in the Gospels (Mt 27:29; Mk 15:17; Jn 19:2), and it makes much more sense given the context. Weaving a plaited crown of thorns requires a great deal of time and a sturdy set of gloves—neither of which the Roman soldiers would probably have had in the middle of this hasty trial.

4. This wine was *posca*, the diluted drink which quenched the thirst of Roman soldiers while allowing their senses to remain sharp. Jesus seems to have drunk the *posca* so that his life could end with a cry of triumph. The wine that Jesus refused when they nailed him to the cross was strong wine, mingled with a drug that would have deadened his senses. According to the rabbis, "when one is led out to execution, he is given a cup of wine, containing frankincense, to numb his senses.... The noble women in Jerusalem used to donate it" (cf. Leon Morris, *The Gospel According to John* [Grand Rapids, Mich.: Eerdmans, 1971], 814).

5. Craig S. Keener, *The IVP Bible Background Commentary* (Downers Grove, Ill.: InterVarsity, 1993), 254.

6. Wangerin, Jr., 121-23.

7. Language alludes to Dietrich Bonhoeffer, *Meditations on the Cross*, ed. and trans. Manfred Weber and D.W. Stott (Louisville: Westminster John Knox, 1998), 25.

8. Tada and Estes, 53-54.

9. This quotation from Psalm 31:5 was part of the liturgy for the evening sacrifice, offered at the ninth hour (Keener, 255).

10. Manning, *Ruthless Trust: The Ragamuffin's Path to God*, 11-12.

TEN
May the Lord Make His Face to Shine Upon You

1. Luke seems to have drawn an intentional parallel between the benediction of Aaron and Jesus' blessing of the disciples (cf. Joseph Fitzmyer, *The Gospel According to Luke 10-24* [New York: Doubleday, 1985], 1590. In his commentary on the harmony of the Gospels, John Calvin also noted the priestly connotations of Luke's account of the Ascension.
2. In the Psalms, "let your face shine" implies the steadfast love and the salvation of God (see, e.g., Ps 31:16).

AFTERWORD
The Glory of Prayer

1. In John 17:22, notice that the result of the disciples' receiving God's glory is fellowship.
2. See Mt 3:17; Mk 14:36; Jn 14:16; Rom 8:26-27.
3. Quoted in Willimon and Hauerwas, 109.

Abba (Aramaic term for father) No precise English equivalent exists for this word which children and adults alike used to address their fathers. It is more intimate than "father," yet more reverent than "daddy."

Adonai (Hebrew, "Lord") Term for a divine ruler, used in the Hebrew Scriptures to refer to God. In prayers and in Scripture readings, *Adonai* frequently functioned as a substitute for the unspeakably holy name of God, *Yahweh*.

Amidah (Hebrew, "standing") Central prayer in Jewish synagogue service. Also known as the *Shemoneh Esrei* ("Eighteen") because, by the late first century, the prayer included eighteen benedictions.

barukh (Hebrew, "blessed," from the root *brkh*) "To bless" or "to bow the knee."

Birkat Ha-Mazon (Hebrew, "blessing of the meal") Jewish prayer recited after every meal. The first-century form of the prayer included three parts—the *birkat hazan* (recognizing that God gives bread to the world), the *birkat ha-aretz* (thanking God for the land of Israel), and the *birkat Yerushalayim* (thanking God for Jerusalem and entreating God to send the Messiah).

charoset Mixture of fruit, nuts, and wine, eaten during the Passover celebration to remind Jews of the mortar that they made when they were slaves in Egypt. Jesus probably dipped the bread that he handed to Judas into the *charoset* (Jn 13:26).

chazan (or, **hazan**) Person in charge of the scrolls in an ancient Jewish synagogue (see Lk 4:17–20). In contemporary Judaism, the *chazan* leads the congregation in prayer.

chatan Jewish bridegroom

cheder (Hebrew, "room" or "chamber") Place where the bride and groom consummated their marriage.

chuppah The canopy under which a Jewish bride and groom are married.

hallel (Hebrew, "praise God") Usually refers to Psalms 113–118, throughout which praising God is a key theme.

Kaddish (or **Qaddish**) (Aramaic, "holy") Aramaic prayer recognizing the holiness of God's name, prayed at the end of the synagogue service and at funerals.

kallah Jewish bride

karpas (Hebrew, "vegetable") Bitter herbs eaten during the Passover meal, to bring to mind the bitterness of the Israelites' slavery in Egypt.

matza, matzoh (Hebrew, "bread") Unleavened bread, traditionally served at Passover.

Messiah (or **Moshiach**) (Hebrew, "anointed one") The redeemer of Israel, promised in the Hebrew Scriptures. "Christ" is the equivalent term in Greek.

Mishnah Traditional interpretations and expansions of the Torah. The Mishnah remained an oral tradition until the second century A.D., when Rabbi Judah Ha-Nasi compiled the oral traditions in written form.

Passover (In Hebrew, **pesach,** "bypassing") Celebration, beginning on the fourteenth of Nisan in the Jewish calendar, celebrating the night when the angel of death passed over the houses of the Jews during their time of slavery in Egypt (see Ex 12:13).

Pentecost (In Hebrew, **shavu'ot,** "fifty days") Celebration of the harvest of the firstfruits of the crops. Begins fifty days after the second day of the Passover festival.

pidyon haben (Hebrew, "redemption of the son") Release of a firstborn son from his responsibility to serve as a priest in the temple. See Numbers 8:14-18.

rabbi A teacher recognized as having the insight to make decisions on issues of Jewish law.

Seder ("order") The ritual followed when commemorating the Passover in a Jewish home.

Shema (Hebrew, "hear") The central Jewish confession of faith, based on Deuteronomy 6:4-9.

sheliach tsibbur (Hebrew, "messenger of the congregation") Individual chosen to expound the Scriptures in a synagogue service.

sheva b'rakhot (Hebrew, "seven blessings") Blessings spoken at a Jewish wedding.

synagogue (Greek, "assembly") Place designated for Jews to worship together and to study the Scriptures. Synagogues arose after the Babylonians destroyed the temple in 586 B.C. Even after the exile ended and the temple was rebuilt, synagogues continued to be central to the Jews' religious lives.

tallith Fringed shawl, worn during morning prayer service. The fringes were intended to fulfill the commandment of God found in Numbers 15:38.

tebhah (Hebrew, "ark") The chest in a synagogue in which the sacred scrolls of Scripture were kept. Also known as the *aron haqqodesh* ("the holy chest").

tefilah (Hebrew, literally "discernment") General term for prayer. When capitalized, *Tefilah* refers to the *Amidah*.

tefillin Small pouches containing passages of Scripture which Jews affix to their foreheads and hands in literal obedience to Exodus 13:9. Also known as "phylacteries" (Mt 23:5).

Torah (Hebrew, "instruction") The first five books of the Hebrew Scriptures—Genesis, Exodus, Leviticus, Numbers, and Deuteronomy.

Yahweh (Hebrew, related to *ehyeh,* "I am") The unspeakable name of God, rooted in Moses' encounter with God at the burning bush (Ex 3:14), usually rendered "LORD" in English Bibles.